# ANTHOLOGY OF POETRY
## BY
## YOUNG AMERICANS®

## 2001 EDITION
## VOLUME XCII

Published by Anthology of Poetry, Inc.

©*Anthology of Poetry by Young Americans*®
2001 Edition
Volume XCII

All Rights Reserved©

Printed in the United States of America

To submit poems
for consideration in the year 2002 edition of the
*Anthology of Poetry by Young Americans*®,
send to: poetry@asheboro.com or

      Anthology of Poetry, Inc.
      PO Box 698
      Asheboro, NC 27204-0698

Authors responsible
for originality of poems submitted.

The Anthology of Poetry, Inc.
307 East Salisbury • P.O. Box 698
Asheboro, NC    27204-0698

Paperback ISBN: 1-883931-27-4
Hardback ISBN: 1-883931-28-2

*Anthology of Poetry by Young Americans*®
is a registered trademark of
Anthology of Poetry, Inc.

For many years now the Anthology of Poetry, Inc. has published the collective insights of the youth of America. Through their written observations they have asked us to connect with them, savor the moment, be lifted by their words, and take heart in the stories they tell us. Fortified with the insights of our young we are prepared to travel ever on to experience the joys of this wonderful life. When we've listened quietly we have learned how they view themselves as well as what we can do to help them on their way. The poems of our children open the doors to their hearts and signal us to the importance of the moment at hand, making us at once student and teacher. Is it any wonder they sometimes lead the way?

We tried to present the poems as the author wrote them, in their format and punctuation. We would like to extend a special thanks to all the poets who participated. We are expecting great things from them in the future.

The Editors

Quiet; listen, hear the truth --
Dwell in the silence forever.
The calamities falsify the calm so preached
Allowing the possible breach of faith.
Unlikely is the total peace
As was never experienced before;
Become accustomed to the unmerry din
Not having to embrace the turbulence within.
Welcome, however, the loudness of the dark;
Secure in the intrigue of mystery
<Merely guidelines offered,
Not instructions.
No "musts", only "maybes"
Just suggestions.>
See inside --
Examine the depths:
One by one, each is to be fully tasted;
The barely perceptible
Are always the most sought after,
Full of flavor.
Savor these --
They seduce the senses.
Learn them --
Judge not their stability
Yet examine their luxuriant fragility;
Tend to them until, fully strengthened,
From within, to out,
They pierce the mob
And win -- for you.

Rachelle Siemasz
Age: 16

M ath is hard that you can see.
A complication it can be.
T he operations you will learn them all.
H urry now and learn them all you cannot afford to stall.

Jeff Donaldson
Age: 11

## SUCCESS

S omeone who accomplishes their goals.
U nderstand your work and assignments.
C ome on you can do it!
C an't you try your best!
E veryone can accomplish their goals if they try!
S tudying is the best thing to do!
S uccess is something everyone can achieve.

Darene Moqbel
Age: 11

# IF I WERE IN CHARGE OF THE WORLD

If I were in charge of the world
There would be longer electives
and a longer lunch hour
Our holidays would be longer
There would be no such word as homework
Everybody would like each other
Kids would get a laptop and a cell phone for free
We would get a free trip around the world
There would be a built-in theme park
in the school

If I were in charge of the world
There would be no such thing a chores,
things would take care of themselves
I would get a 1,000,000,000,000,000 allowance
each week
We would have a built-in water park
in the basement
We would live on eighty acres of land
We would eat the top-of-the-line food
We would give to charity
If I were in charge of the world

Matthew Lambert
Age: 11

# CHRISTMASTIME

I love Christmastime
I love to hear the bells chime
Oh, how I love Christmastime
This season comes after Thanksgiving
It's a time for wishing and praising
When the stores put out their decorations
It's a time for jubilation
When the snow falls on a bright winter day
Everybody yells "hooray"
People make nice warm quilts
While snowmen are being built
The kids all bundled up
Come inside to have a cup; of cocoa
Salt is poured on the streets
While people make the sweetest treats
Christmas trees are in the living rooms
With luminous lights
That shine so bright
On Christmas Eve, we gather 'round
With gifts and songs abound
That night, we set out the sweetest treat
And hope that Santa will eat
Boys and girls are asleep in their beds
With dreams of toys in their heads
Santa drops the toys off so quietly at their house
That no one would know he's there
Not even a mouse

Santa leaves with his eight reindeer and sleigh
And everyone wakes up to a wonderful
Christmas Day
They have games, toys, makeup and clothes
Bikes, sleds, and much, much more
But Christmas is something more than that
And that's why I love Christmas so much
It's love, happiness, and glee!!

Kirsten Nowak
Age: 11

## HAPPY

Happy is the color of bright blue.
It sounds like a baby's giggle.
It smells like a rose that just bloomed.
Happy looks like friends laughing together.
Happy tastes like a hot fudge sundae.

Sarah LeBlanc

# BLACK BEAR

There once was a little black bear
Who thought he could fly through the air
When he tried to take flight
He got such a fright
That he fell down and lost all his hair!

Robin Greenwood
Age: 12

# THE ATTIC OF THE WIND

Up in the air
way up there
Where the wind blows
and pulls out your bows.
The air seems to have a collection of things
Even little European bells that ring!
As they fly out of your hand
It's like they're going to another land.
They leap and spin and fly and spin and soar
Things are flying up more and more!
Stuff from all over the world
Is up there being twisted and twirled
It's almost like something magic
You'll see too if you go to the wind's attic!

Julia McLean
Age: 9

## MY FAT GUINEA PIG

My fat guinea pig
He jumps around and does a jig
He eats a lot he gets big
I can't believe he can even dig

Zachary Turbin
Age: 8


## THE DREAM

Flying away from all the world's troubles
Dreaming I'm floating inside of a bubble
Looking down upon the earth's face
Flying away at a steady pace
Away from all the mountains of rubble

Floating up to a sunny place
A world of waterfalls, beauty, and grace
With streets of gold
And beauty so bold
Where trouble disappears without a trace

Sad to leave such a happy place
I fall back to earth at a rapid pace
Slicing through clouds like they are butter
Slowing down I start to flutter
Back to reality filled with grace

Cory Simonds

# MY LITTLE SISTER

My little sister is mad
When she doesn't get food she's sad
Most of the time she's bad
But when Dad comes around she's glad

Christopher White
Age: 7

# CATS

Cats always sleep
They always weep
They sleep in a jeep
They sleep by the heat
They sit in a seat.

Kevin Glegola

# CHAIRS

You sit in a chair
When you write a poem
You sit in a chair
When you ride a bus home
You sit in a chair
When you put on your shoes
You sit in a chair
When you watch the news

Rory Smith
Age: 9

# TO BE THE PRESIDENT

I wish I could be the president
Though I am only ten
My papa is the president
And so was my uncle Ben
Papa says to be president
I have to be much bigger and older
Since then it's been two weeks
And I'm not even up to Papa's shoulder
It would take so very long to be
Just like Papa and Uncle Ben
Then suddenly it came to me
That I am still only ten.

Andy Bahena
Age: 11

## DAD

When Dad was a wee lad
he was bad,
but never sad.
He had a black cat
that sat on a mat
and was really fat.
Dad had a little girl
who had a pearl
who knew how to twirl.
He had a little boy
who had a toy.
The boy played with the toy
in joy.
Dad was glad,
he was no longer bad.

Ashley Theisen
Age: 10


## DANCE

There was a ghost in France.
This ghost liked to dance.
She liked to dance all day.
She liked to dance in May.
She liked to dance with a boy named Lance.

Brittany Marie Rich Kusiak
Age: 9

# TURTLES

Turtles lay their eggs
They walk on all four legs.
Under the water they sleep
The water is very, very deep.
Turtles can swim
They can swim with Kim.

Katie Smith
Age: 8

# PIZZA

Pizza is good
It does not taste like wood
The best part of pizza is cheese
Can I have a double-cheese pizza.
Please.

Leah Bauer

# SUNLIGHT

Beautiful sunlight
Covers the wonderful trees
With your stunning rays

Jessica Anne Golich
Age: 11

# SNOWFLAKES

Snowflakes fall on a cloudy day,
While children inside want to play,
They look out a window,
And saw snowflakes fall one by one,
Until they saw it hit the ground,
They wanted to go outside and play in the snow,
But it snowed too hard and their mother said no,
They looked outside and started to stare,
Because other children were playing there,
It falls and falls but it cannot stop,
It got so boring,
Until they matched each snowflake up,
When they got tired and they didn't bare,
And went to sleep without a care,
It falls and falls but it cannot stop,
Until the morning when they got up,
They went outside without a doubt,
Until it got dark
And they thought it was enough for...
... Those wonderful snowflakes.

Denah Farhat
Age: 12

# GRANDMA'S WORDS

I sit here,
Trying to hold my tears.
I helplessly watch her lie there,
Nothing I can do.
She is sicker than I've ever seen,
My grandma.
She has always told me,
"Remember in every hardship
you can get through it with your heart."
As she whispers faintly,
Those are her words now.
What will I do
without my loving caring inspiration?
I cannot live without her.
I will never get that special big bear hug,
Or that soft warm kiss on my cheek.
She is gone,
She is dead,
She has left me 'til the day I die.
I cannot bear this pain hitting my heart.
How will I survive this?
That is all I can think over and over again.
Then I remember Grandma's loving words,
Now when I think of Grandma,
I think of,
Big bear hugs,
Soft warm kisses,
And the smile I used to give my grandma,
Comes to my face once more.

Candace Edwards

# HALLOWEEN NIGHT

H alloween is a spooky night
A nd gives kids a fearsome fright
L ots of
L aughing all night long until a ghost comes along
O ften children run away
W ith the ghost all the way
E vil spirits come and go
E verybody got the flow
N ow Halloween is all done now we can have some fun

Chelsea Butera
Age: 9


# MEMORIES

Memories, memories.
Memories are with you.
Every move you make.
Even with every photo you look at.
Memories will never leave you.
Memories are like a shadow.
A very special shadow
that will never leave your side.
Never forget those special memories
that will never leave you.


Ashley Gaumer
Age: 11

# WHAT IS ORANGE?

Orange is the color of leaves in fall.
Orange is the color of a basketball.
Orange is my most favorite color of all.

Orange is the color of the summer sun.
It's the color of the sky when the day is done.
Orange is bright, cheerful, and fun.

Orange is the mixture of yellow and red.
Orange is the color of the sheet on my bed.
Orange is the hair on Michael Hool's head.

Orange is the color of flames
  growing bigger and bigger.
Orange is the color of the bouncing Tigger.
Orange is the color of an orange -- go figure!

Christina Butler
Age: 11

# THE RHYME

I hear the music and I know it's time,
To dance my poem; my flowing rhyme,
I make it up as I go along,
I weave my way through colorful songs.

Lisa Marija Geldys

# WHAT IS BLUE?

Blue is my color.
It's my favorite, it's true.
Do you have a color
  that you like too?

Blue socks, sky, blueberries,
   just to name a few.
My mom has one brown and one blue.

Blue I feel when I am mad
  and don't know what to do.
I hold my breath
  'til I turn blue.

Blue feeling I get
  When I fail a test
When I do my best
  Wouldn't you?

Blue is the bluebird
  I see every day
Why he returns
  I really can't say.

Blue is my uncle Boo
  who has to go to the hospital
  to repair a hernia or two.
He'll feel better when it's through.

Blue is the ice
   where Nicholas skates.
He is a goalie
   winning his fate.

Blue jays are a baseball team.
Where the crowds like to scream.
They hope to win
   that's their dream.

Blue and gold
   are my school colors.
I'm proud to wear them
   to show how I feel to others.

Blue heavens above,
   I show God my love
   by doing my very best
   by not following the rest.

Blue is a peaceful color
   it makes you feel great.
It's part of our flag
   that stands for our fifty states.

Blue expresses a color
   or a feeling that's sad.
If it didn't exist
   I'd be really mad.

Nicholas Armbruster
Age: 11

# ORANGE IS...

Orange is the sunrise bright and strong.
Orange is dried grass in the hot summer.
Orange is the autumn leaves
  running across the lawn.
Orange is happiness filling in my mind.
Orange is the brave spot in my soul.
Orange is a pumpkin at Halloween.
Orange is an orange marker
  gliding across the paper.
Orange is the sunset happy that the day is over.
Orange is the best in the west
  and it's my favorite of all.
Orange is the color of my mom's dress.
Orange is the color of my dad's face
  when he is mad.
Orange can describe many things
  and many things is what orange describes.

T. J. Gosselin
Age: 12


# RUDE

Rude is the taste of a sour pickle.
It sounds like someone who doesn't look good.
And smells like a dead rat.
Rude looks like someone eating in front of someone.
It makes me feel dirty.
And rude is the color brown.

Joél Gonzalez
Age: 11

# WORK THEN REST

Squirrels gather nuts,
In the summertime of year,
Rest is in winter.

Adam Ourchane
Age: 11

# WHAT IS BLACK

Black is the evil
that is inside of you.
Black is the chalkboard,
that runs wall to wall.

Black is the clock
that we look at all day
Black is the TV
that we sit in front of.

Black is the crow
that eats our crops
Black is the smoke
that we breathe in all the time.

Black is the dark
where we watch our scariest movies
Black is selfish
he has a death wish.

Kyle Zarem
Age: 12

# GREEN IS...

Green is the grass,
Vivid and keen.
Green is the earth,
Trying to keep clean.

Green is go,
Letting you know.
Green is the bright stars,
Outlining the constellations they know.

Green is a map,
With a big mount.
Green is the money,
In your account.

Green is the clouds
Bearing tornadoes.
Green is a book,
Telling what it knows.

Green is Peter Pan,
Saving the day.
Green is the stems,
In April and May.

Green is a snake,
Ready to strike.
Green is a lake,
And even your bike.

Green is the earth,
No doubt about it.
But can you imagine,
Living without it?

Logan Bonathan
Age: 11


## HAPPINESS

Happiness sounds like birds chirping
It tastes like sweet melted chocolate
It smells like hot cocoa by a fire
Happiness looks like beautiful swans in a pond
It makes me feel wonderful

Josephine Berry
Age: 11


## THE GIRL NAMED PEARL

Here is a girl named Pearl
She liked a guy named Earl
Her hair was so straight
So up-to-date
Then it began to curl

Cassandra Shamey

# WHAT IS SILVER?

Silver is a crisp snowfall,
   glistening in the morning.
Silver is a beautiful crystal lake,
   cool and calm.
Silver is a small dog,
   with brilliantly shining fur.
Silver is a piece of a memory,
   shining bright and clear.

Silver is a reflection,
   of God's brilliant beauty.
Silver is a ringing bell,
   loud for all to hear.
Silver is a mellow color,
   calming your mind.
Silver is a shimmering dime
   flashing in the light.
Silver paints very little in our huge world.
The world favors other colors.
Hues of red and blue.
But silver is my favorite color,
   how about you?

Matthew J. Ketchum
Age: 11

# PERIWINKLE

Periwinkle is like fairies,
It's so sweet and delicate, with dainty wings.

Periwinkle is like the sky,
Stretching around the entire world,
Loving it as a child.

Periwinkle is peaceful and calm,
Like the ocean waves
against a sandy, golden beach.

Periwinkle is a crayon,
Giving color to everything.
It is a new beginning,
Starting each spring,
Just when all the birds start to sing.

Periwinkle is gentle and comforting,
Like a mother singing to a sleepy child.

Periwinkle is a charming shade of blue,
And without it, what would we do?

Andrea Posh
Age: 11

# WHAT'S GOLDENROD

Goldenrod is bright,
You can see it at night.
Goldenrod is yellow's brother.
But to gold she's a mother.
Goldenrod plays a nice soft tune.
Not like the drums or the bassoon.
Goldenrod flashes light very quick.
A lot bigger flash than a candlestick.
Goldenrod is cheese.
Hard not to please.
Goldenrod is far and near.
But imagine it not being here.

Eric Jacovetti
Age: 11

# MY MOM

My mom is nice
She eats rice
She is nicer than my dad
Even when she is mad
She has dice
And eats ice
Because she is nice.

MacKenzie Theisen
Age: 7

# MY COUSIN ROY

Christmas is full of joy,
Just like a happy boy.
If you get a toy,
It may be from my cousin, Roy.

Roy is always glad,
Even when you get mad.
Don't get sad,
Because Roy may get mad.

Roy gives gifts,
That are hard to lift.
Don't try to give a fit,
Or you won't get a gift.

Victoria Dylegowski
Age: 11

# PARENTS

P arents are good
A lways there for you
R eading you a book
E very night
N ever giving up
T eaching you lots of things
S aying I love you each day

Rochelle Polskoy
Age: 8

# WHAT IS TEAL?

Teal is a mixture of blues and greens.
Teal is the color of the ocean, very calm.
Teal is in the sunset.
Teal is the color of a summer's sky.
Teal is as cute as a baby seal.
Teal is the color of the ribbon she ties in her hair.
Teal is the color of the lace on her dress.
Teal is the color of the girl scout uniform.
Teal is the color of the egg the robin lays.
Teal is the color of the bow
    on her birthday package.
Teal is the color of her grandmother's
    glistening eyes.
Teal is the color of the flower
    on the gift she received.
Teal is a very special color.
The world would be dull without teal.

Annette DiCello
Age: 11

# MY PLAYSTATION

Oh, PlayStation, oh, PlayStation!
I love my PlayStation.
All I do is play my PlayStation.
I play it all I can
Until someone turns it off and I say
HEY!

Tanyon Valentine
Age: 9

# WHAT IS YELLOW?

Yellow is the sunrise waiting for you to wake up.
Yellow is the star
   that you put on your Christmas tree.
Yellow is the stars shining down on us.
Yellow is the moon giving us light at night.

Yellow is the color of leaves in the fall.
Yellow is the color of a flower in the spring.
Yellow is the color of a bus going to school.

Yellow is happiness.
Yellow reminds me of the star
   when Jesus was born.
Yellow is the feeling of a newborn baby.
Yellow makes me feel grateful
   when I see how much I have.
Yellow is very mellow
   it makes me feel comfortable.

I wonder what the world would be like
   without yellow!

Kaitlin Waldecker
Age: 11

# WHAT IS GREEN?

Green is great,
Green is good,
Green is in our neighborhood.
Green is the grass that grows in our yard,
Green can be soft, flat, fertile, or hard.

Green is the light that tells us to go.
People obey it to go with the flow.
The prettiest color I've ever seen,
Is the color you spend; it's the color green.

Green is a color of Christmas so fun,
I'm gonna ask my parents
    for a green paintball gun.
Green is the Christmas tree
    on our living room floor,
Green is the wreath hanging on our front door.

Green are the lights we put up each year,
Green is the Grinch that all kids fear.
Mixing colors are fun to do,
To make green you mix yellow and blue.

Colin Marquardt
Age: 12

# WHAT IS BLUE?

Blue is a big balloon,
Flying in the air.

Blue is the sadness
That bursts from your eyes.

Blue is the wind in the sky.
Howling in the night.

Blue is the sea.
It's baking up a storm.

Blue is a bluebird,
Streaming through the sky.

Blue is a beachball
Beating in the air.

Blue is a babbling
Blue-footed booby.

Blue is my favorite color.
And I love blue.

Lisa Salaita
Age: 11

Summer folds around me.
It grabs me by the hands
and puts lighting electricity through my blood.
I spin.

You press me down now.
My arms twist unnaturally in struggle.
Maybe it is right, maybe for my spoken thoughts
To hatch their way through the wire and sheets.

Although summer exists unchanged
and it differs not from that
twelve months previous,
Now I feel it
it's transcendence of season.

Let me go.
You may say I choose my capture.
Convince me, then, to forget,
To lose you in reasons.

Here I connect with you,
with life, with trees bearing crisp teethy leaves,
They sway and dangle nudged by the wind
Pale skies make me tired.

Your words are summer
which lies down for autumn.
Escapable as you are I rush through things
and still drag
Anchored by a surge within me.

Alison R. Nawrocki
Age: 16

# ZOOP

There once was a pilot named Zoop
Who's plane got a hole like a hoop
He jumped out to cry
He saw a cow pie
Then poor Zoop landed in...

Noah Polakowski Keelan
Age: 11

# SILVER'S GLORIES

Silver is a dove flying gracefully in the sky.

Silver is the scales of a wondrous snake
    not to mention a crystal-clear lake.
Silver is my grandpa's silky hair.
Silver are the trees so bare.

Silver is a color that represents magic.
Silver is a color that is never tragic!
Silver is the glistening snow.
Silver is a color with a beautiful glow!

Silver is my bracelet, so elegant with delight.
Silver is a color that can say "Good night"
Silver is the moon, so brilliant and bright.
Silver is the color that fits me just right.

Christina Fitzpatrick
Age: 12

# WHAT IS BLACK?

Black is the color of the night sky
  so big and wide,
Black consumes everything in its path
  on a moonless night.

Black makes you think of a deep damp cellar
  blinded with darkness,
Black fills up the tiniest spaces,
Black makes the black cat's eyes
  stand out like a beacon on a dark eerie night.

Black is the mournful color of death and dismay,
Black is a dreadful color
  making you lost and disoriented.

Black is also a very peaceful color
  letting you look up at the stars with a blanket
  of black velvet covering them from danger
Black is the color of water deep with curiosity
  and fear, waiting to take you away.

Black is the dress of a dancing maiden
  twirling around.
When you despise someone
  black has control of your mind.

Black likes to have races with the light
   to see who's faster.
A world without black is boring and dull,
   without it the world would have no night
   and no fear.

Wouldn't you agree?

Hannah Diebel
Age: 11

## BLACK

Black is evil it gives great fright.
Black is dark and is the night.
When it's black it is quiet,
   nothing like a loud riot.

Black is my shadow mimicking me.
Black is so dark you cannot see.
Black is the color of some people's hair,
   swaying badly in the bright air.

Bad luck is found in a stack,
where you walk by a cat that's black
So be careful what you write,
   it might give you a fright.

Joe Marino
Age: 12

# IMPERFECTIONS

In the mirror.
I see these imperfections.
Yet they aren't me,
They aren't real.
Let's say they were placed there
By an evil sorcerer
To hide the beauty inside.
All but my eyes,
Windows to the world inside,
If any care to look,
Through the brown windows,
To perfection,
That is the soul inside.

Crystal Cloke
Age: 14


# LOVE

Love is the wonderful color of red
It sounds like beautiful romantic music
It tastes like dark chocolate Hershey Kisses
It smells like roses blooming in the soft air
Love looks like a red silky dress
It makes you feel wonderful

Angie Colón
Age: 11

# MILKY WAY

It is in the sky
We live in the Milky Way
Milky Way is large.

Lindsey Stark
Age: 8

# CORNFLOWER

Cornflower is the flowers in the field.
Cornflower is that one dress you love.
Cornflower dwells with the angels above.
Cornflower can grow next to an oak.
Cornflower is the queen of all saints cloak.
Cornflower is a magic enchantment,
Cornflower is peaceful and quiet.
If you could feel cornflower
 it would feel like a very soft powder.
When you draw with a cornflower crayon,
 it seems as if it goes with almost
 any other crayon.
If I lose my cornflower crayon
 I'm going to start a riot.  (Just kidding)
If you cold taste cornflower
 it would taste like a soft biscuit
 with melting margarine on top.
Cornflower is mostly never thought of,
But gifted by God, just the same.

Anne Christine Avian
Age: 11

# NEVER AGAIN WILL I BE A PLAIN GIRL!

Never again I saw my fear
of being haunted by my love .
The fever began to rush into my brain full of sin.
Lynn was my middle name but it felt like my first.
I rose and began to feel like
an African queen of glory in my sight.
I was never again a regular girl.
I was special to me in my  heart and in history.
I'll be known as Queen Alistina forever
until no more of me.

Lajoya Rush
Age: 11

# WHAT IS GOLD?

Gold is the star on a Christmas tree,
Gold is the sun setting over the sea.
Gold is the color of angels' wings,
Gold is the key that opens things.
Gold is the crown that is worn by a king,
Gold is a locket, a necklace, or ring.
Gold is the coin you drop in a well,
Gold is a secret you'll never tell.
Gold is a medal, a first place prize.
Gold is the look in your puppy's eyes.
Gold is a feeling, a color, a friend,
Like the pot of gold at the rainbow's end.

Mary DeCelle
Age: 11

# FRIENDS

A friend is like a fork in the road,
Leading to the good and the bad,
A friend is like an animal,
Don't give them too much freedom,
Or they'll push you around.

The earth,
The galaxy,
The whole universe,
Would be nothing,
Without friends.

Matthew Jacob Villa
Age: 11


# THE SCHOOL

I go to Gudith School

And I think it's really cool
We have a very nice teacher
She deals with all us creatures.

What I really like is lunch
All the goodies that I munch
And my friends are really neat
As long as they don't eat  my treat.

Jodie Clark
Age: 7

Shining yellow star
Floating softly in the sky
Tiny speck of light.

Carolyn Zick
Age: 9

## WHAT IS ORANGE?

Orange is the color of my bright hair,
Orange is the color of a burning flare.
Orange is the color of a boiling stove,
Orange is the freckles on my nose.

Orange is the sun, blazing and hot,
Orange is the color of my mom's cooking pot.
Orange is the color of a basketball,
Orange is the color of leaves in the fall.

Orange is the color of a June night sky,
Orange is the color of my favorite tie.
Orange is my favorite color of all,
The color of orange is the best of all.

Michael Hool
Age: 11

When the sun goes down
And the stars begin to shine
The moon shows his face

Allie Harris
Age: 9


## WHAT IS YELLOW?

Yellow is the beautiful sun,
Shining so lovely until the day is done.
Yellow is the stars, shining brightly
Looking over us as we sleep quietly
Yellow is a lemon, sour and tart
Yellow is a beautiful piece of art.
Yellow is a newborn baby duck
Yellow is a charm used for good luck.
Yellow is a buzzing bee
Yellow is the leaves in the fall
    that come from a tree.
I love yellow, yes it's true,
I love yellow, how about you?

Molly Pastula
Age: 12

Cheetah,
very fast,
running, sleeping, eating,
legs, mouth, ears, trunk,
eating, washing, sleeping,
very big,
Elephant

Gabriel Achilli Helmuth
Age: 10

Skier
graceful, beautiful.
gliding, swooshing, skiing.
skis, boots, skiers, mountain.
shining, glistening, sparkling.
cold, white.
Snow

Michaela Wood

Michael
Basketball
Tall, plays basketball, record of shots
and best basketball player ever
Lover of basketball, kids and golf
He believed he could be
the best basketball player
Who wanted to play for North Carolina,
baseball and the Bulls
Who used a basketball, jersey and Nike shoes
Who gave help, peace and harmony
Who said, "Always do your best."
Jordan

Luke Salchert
Age: 9

## YELLOW

Yellow is full of joy.
Just like a ten-year-old boy.
Yellow is the stars that lead us through the night.
Yellow is the sun that gives us light.
Yellow is a piece of macaroni.
Feeling very lonely.
Yellow is very sorrowful.
Also very powerful.
I think about yellow for a half of an hour.
Yellow is a lemon that's very sour.
Yellow should be with us all our life.
Even when I have a wife.

Weston Dwight
Age: 11

# WHY DID THEY DO THIS TO ME?

I woke up yesterday morning
  to the sound of screaming and gunshots.
Who would do this to me?
Who would do this to us?

I had lived in the ghetto now for one week.
How could they do this to me?
How could they do this to us?

They herded us into a cargo train,
  where we were packed less than inches
  from each other.
What made them do this to me?
What made them do this to us?

For three days I suffered that awful train ride.
Why did they do this to me?
Why did they do this to us?

When we stopped,
  we were taken to the large "showers."
Where was their heart
  when they were doing this to me?
Where was their heart
  when they were doing this to us?

When we huddled in and turned them on,
  out came poisonous gas.
When were they going to stop doing this to me?
When were they going to stop doing this to us?

Our loved ones, friends, and many others
   drifted out of the incinerators
   as the smell of burning flesh
   and thick, black smoke.
Why did they do this to me?
Why did they do this to us?

I will tell you why they did it to us.
We are Jewish.

Ellen West
Age: 13

## PENGUINS DANCING

Penguins dancing in the sea
Penguins dancing you can see.
Me and my uncle flew here in a helicopter.
You can see a penguin do a belly flopper.
Now I must go into the yonder
But my thoughts are still a flonder.

Ryan Weir Smith
Age: 10

# DRAGONFLY

As I watch a dragonfly
Zooming through the macrocosm
Just passing by
I wonder about their simple life
To live, mate, and die
Our lives are so complicated,
It causes me to sigh

If only we were like the winged insect
So easy in everyway
They take on living with nothing to reject
We worry about pollution,
Technology, and school
And yet, maybe it is we who are the fools

Dragonflies don't have to be intelligent
To have success
In our world, we need to be smart
To even think about wealth
We have made human existence a gigantic mess
Not enough of us feel sympathy,
Compassion, or joy
Is someone just rendering us like a toy?

In order to solace the efforts of the day
We could at least stop and watch for a moment
The dragonflies at play
To see how different their lives are
Would be an improvement in the human's mind,
Holding it ajar

Darcy Nicole Wallace
Age: 12

## GOALIE

The puck slides back,
You hear a crack.
You try to block the shot.
It hits your pad, it hits your stick.
It slides past the line.

Aaron Francis
Age: 11


## GOOD-BYE

When you say good-bye
even if you have planned
the departure for years,
that doesn't even begin to stop
the ever-so-fast coming tears.
Then you see flashbacks
of your happy and joyful past,
and then you just wish
them forever to last.
Your mind makes playback
as they slowly float away,
and then you wish
they were forever here to stay.
It's like they held
a special piece of your heart,
and then as they leave
you feel it slowly break apart.

Katelin Music
Age: 11

# WHY?

Why am I here?
My life is blank and senseless
and seems to have no end!
Even though I'm young
I still have stress days
and heartbreaks and pains
from the loss of loved ones
that I just can't seem to put to an end.

Why don't you set me free
from what seems to be an everlasting life!
Sometimes I feel like my heart has been
ripped out of my chest
and stabbed by a thousand knives
and I feel myself slowly slipping away!
When I realize that I had not died
I wish that I had.

When people try to say
it's going to be all right
their words are bare without meaning
like an old abandoned building
somewhere far and lost!

Ashley Renee McGuire
Age: 12

# FAY

There once was a bird named Fay.
She was always very gay.
She fell on her shoe
and landed, "Boohoo"
Now she is sad all day.

Stephanie Pearl
Age: 11


## THE NIGHT OF THE BUSH MONKEY

Monkey see
Monkey do.
Monkeys hide
In bushes too.
You can ask
A McDonald's fry.
She stared at
The monkey eye-to-eye.
The monkey chased
A very ecstatic,
Screeching, yelling
Eric Craddock.
The monkey makes
People scream.
On the night of
HALLOWEEN!!!

Jacob Brewer
Age: 12

# DEATH

It was the last day of school.
We all had a picnic.
I heard some girl squeal out loud
"Call an ambulance."
I asked my friend Erin what had happened,
Erin said she had a seizure.
Some boy came up to me
and said that she had just passed out.
I never did find out what had happened for sure.
It really made me think it could have been me.
I've always had medical problems.
Then that made me think even more
we are all going to DIE.

Briana Daggett
Age: 12

# HOLIDAYS

Holidays are chock-full of glee and cheer.
Holidays are when you spend time with your family.
Holidays are for gift giving.
Holidays are for feasts.
Holidays are joyous.
Holidays are for decorating.
Holidays make family memories of joy.

Jessica Kirkwood
Age: 12

# BEST FRIEND

Best friend?
What exactly do those two words mean?
A best friend is a person who sticks up for you.
And when you are feeling down
they cheer you up.
A best friend is a person
that you can tell her anything.
And you can trust them.
She always encourages me to do my schoolwork.
She believes that I can do good.
Lauren McNicol is my best friend.
We hang out all the time.
We have tons and tons of memories.
She is the funniest, kindest,
most caring person I ever met.
She puts other people first before herself.
If I need something she will let me use it.
I've only known her for two years
and we've hung out ever since.
So when you think you found your best friend,
don't ever lose them.
Lauren is my best friend.

Joanna Krystyan
Age: 13

# RUNNING AWAY

She thought it was right at the time,
but she didn't know
who she was leaving behind.
Her family and friends all understood,
her life of living under a hood.
So here she was in the rain all alone,
thinking of her family safe at home.
She decided her life was not on the right track,
so then decided to turn back.
She saw her mother from a kitchen window,
and realized then just how much she missed her.
She saw her sister  in her bedroom weeping,
and to the door she started creeping.
It was late at night
when she walked through the door,
her family came running
their tears started to pour.
At last she was home safe in bed,
she swore to her family never to run away again.

Kristina Koons
Age: 13

## THE '68 CAMARO

My beloved car is a '68 Camaro.
My admired color for this car is blue
I like the sharp look of this car too.
The thing I like about this car
is it is swift and cool.
Please don't crash these classic cars
because they rule.

Michael B. Courtney
Age: 14

## THANKSGIVING, THANKSGIVING

Thanksgiving,
Thanksgiving is the life we're living.
Watching snow melt at my toe.
Cranberries, cherries, turkeys and berries.
Family galore animals and more.
We sit by the fire while we all are very tired.
Eating pie licking the pan dry.

Jordan Malos

# FOOTBALL

The coach sends me out there
I thought boy what a scare.
We're playing against the Woodhaven Knights
with their spacious bodies and tall in height.

In the huddle tense to the bone
wishing I was home.
In formation waiting for him to say the words
he says when we are doing a play.

He gives the ball away to me
as the ball gets stolen
as the coach shouts at me.

Antoine L. Byse<br>
Age: 14

# CHRISTMAS MORNING

I woke up and looked out my window,
The snow was falling all around,
I walked down the stairs without a frown,
I knew there were presents all around,
The trees, the lights, the wrapping paper,
Were beautiful in their sight,
I opened my gifts,
And played with them until Christmas night.

Joe Stull<br>
Age: 14

## MS. POPULAR

I broke out of my shell today
all my fears have gone away
the deception that my peers have given
I put aside, my own decision
I'll be in no clique, be in no class
sure, to you this may sound crass
but underneath your thick persona
someone's in there, abracadabra
poof, you've always been in there
yes, it's you and you shouldn't care
what people say 'bout what you do
you should tell them," I'm me, you're you."
I used to wonder from day-to-day
what they'd think if I wasn't their way
then realized I felt alone
tired of staring at the phone
waiting for "Ms. Popular" to call
then we'd go shopping for her at the mall
I saw my wrong, and believe me --
it took me quite some time to see
you know what you have to do
prove that who you are is you
well now I'm done and hope you realize
please don't change to fit in their eyes

Sarah Wielusz
Age: 16

# THE MALL

The mall is filled with many things
Things I can't explain
The mall is filled with many colors
Colors like blue and gray
The mall is filled with many people
People like you and me
The mall is filled with many clothes
Clothes like shirts and shorts
The mall is filled with many stores
Stores like Gap and Claire's
But I guess I'm acting a little funny
Because I wish I had some money!

Susannah Harrington
Age: 11


My favorite sport is hockey.
I choose hockey
because there is a lot of fighting.
I prefer to beat people.
I don't know why,
I just do.
I have always been a mercenary,
even when I was a baby.
My last appeal would be
to play for the Detroit Red Wings

Joshua Parden
Age: 12

## I LOVE GYMNASTICS

Warmups, stretching, running in place,
Puts a smile on my face.
Tumbling, jumping, cartwheels, too,
Makes me always yell YAHOO!
Vault, mats, bars and beam,
Keeps me moving with lots of steam.
Headstands, handstands and the splits,
V-sits, candlesticks, pullovers and dips.
Backwards, forwards and upside-down,
Gymnastics NEVER makes me frown!

Mallory Kuhr
Age: 6


## MOTHERS

Are there to comfort you,
to be with you and talk to you
You go to bed
thinking of everything you did today
You turn around and just frown,
Your loving mother once alive, died
Her warm hand that once touched yours
is no longer there
You cry all night
just thinking about her kiss on your cheek,
And miss her every week

Jennifer Lynn Smith
Age: 11

# STARING AT ME

As I walk down the school hallway,
everything suddenly paused.
Hi! I recited. No reply.
All I see are eyes staring at me.
I keep walking thinking, what did I do?
Maybe I did something good, and these people
are rewarding me with their smiles.
I look around. No smiling.
I then have thoughts, thinking,
are they staring at me because I look cool?
Or do I look like a big fool?
Or is it because I'm pretty
and they are admiring me?
Or is it because I look deceiving
and they dare to look at me?
Or is it because I smell?
I took a shower this morning
and used deodorant.
The eyes still in my direction.
Do they have a staring problem?
I think to myself.
Because if they do, I know a good eye doctor
who will examine their eyes
for the price of twelve.
Is it because of my uncombed hair?
After all I haven't washed it in over a week.
Is it because of my clothes?
Blue jeans, a tank top,
and a pair of green sneakers?
Take a picture it'll last longer, I wanted to shout.

I also wanted to sit down and pout,
but I had to be a young lady
and stand up for myself.
I can't go out and be a baby.
Oh well, I'll get over this;
I've gotten over many things before.
Like the time I broke my hand
by slamming it in the car door.
All these people might be jealous
of my good looks, intelligence, and style,
but I still get a little nervous
when I walk down the school hall,
and I see eyes staring at me.

Princess Ogundipe
Age: 11


MY DOG

My dog is nice.
Her name is Sam.
She is always there
When I get in a jam.

Walter Polskoy
Age: 8

# HOCKEY IS THE BEST

There is a test
that I like the best.
When playing hockey with the rest,
our team is the best
and will beat the rest.

Ryan Boljesic

# TREES

Trees are beautiful to watch.
Look deeper than the leaves and you'll see,
that trees are old in age,
but they still keep their beauty.
Trees live long and see many faces,
But they do not move to different places.
And in that one place their beauty spreads,
Like butter on a piece of bread.
More trees appear,
Out of nowhere.
When winter comes they all die,
Only to live again to see the animals
and children go by.
Their leaves grow back,
and once again they are free.
Oh, how I wish I were a tree.

Sumeyya Rehman

## SPRING: THE HERO

The elated sun shows off its rays,
  Bursts through the cloud's haze.
The period of waiting undercover,
  Faded away as the sun longed to hover.
Rays spread wide by the shining star,
  Happiness and energy shower by far.
Thou Spring has finally arrived,
  Blessing each flower at every stride.
Ceased were the birds and bees,
  But finally they will be at ease.
O Spring!  Enchanted season,
  You revive and strive for a reason.

Abderrahim Alem
Age: 15


## MY BAD DAY

Sometimes I hate to say
I'm going to have a bad day.
I cry sweet tears
then they fall down my face.
I wish I could have more fun
but the day is still ticking away.
Like I said,
I hate to say I'm going to have a bad day.

Kimisha Patterson
Age: 11

# ORANGE-RED FLOWER

Orange-red flower
It is tanning in the sun
It needs a cold drink

Elizabeth Forester

# SOCCER BALL

I have a ball
In my hand,
It is all shiny and gold.

The ball hangs
Around my neck,
And brings me
Good luck.

It reminds me of
A day, when
We played in
The rain.

It shows me
The way
Down the field.

Cortney Christophel
Age: 11

# LEAVES

The leaves fly by
in all types of shapes.
The leaves dip in the wind
like eggs in eggbeaters.

Jeron K. Johnson Jr.
Age: 9

# JESUS

"Prepare his way," said the prophet John;
"His life among us brings new dawn."
Then to the Jordan Jesus came;
The world will never be the same.

The small child was born on this world,
A divine human being,
His mother, Mary; our Father, the Lord,
Many barn animals all seeing.

Come all ye faithful ones
To Jesus, the Son of God.
Bow down on your knees and suffer none.
Believe in Jesus, the Lamb of God.

He is gone, they thought,
But only his body, Peter knew.
His spirit is with us, weren't you taught?
He has resurrected; His body anew!

Jennie Spencer

# WHO IS GOD?

Who is God?
God is the Father of man.
He built the earth for me and you.
So who is God?

Who is God?
He created me and you.
Who is God?
He gave us a place to learn.
Who is God?
He made us a place to be safe out of harm's way.
Who is God?
He made Heaven.

Who is God?
He is the Father.
Who is God?
God can fix everything.
Who is God?
Leave all your problems with Him
And He will fix it.
Who is God?
Just pray.
Who is God?

Laeishia Johnson
Age: 11

# SHE IS GONE

Like the wind, she is gone.
In my heart she's a song.
That hums and whistles a tune.
I will never forget in the morning,
Or forget in the afternoon.
Time and again I realized
Why she died,
And how I cried.
I shall remember this poem
At school and at home,
And hope that she is reborn.

The silent night,
Gave me a fright.
I could not sleep.
I think of you
And hope my dreams come true.
Make my day fine,
I'll think of you
And my day will shine.

I heard a noise
And hoped it was you.
But it wasn't so I hope and sneeze
Dream and scream.
You are gone.

Fa'Dia Shenya Higgs
Age: 10

# THE 1950'S

Boy 1: I touch the railing as I walk up the stairs
of my new integrated school.
I feel the hatred and fearful eyes
that are looking upon me
as I walk up the school stairs.
I can see the people's disgusted and furious mien.
I can hear the horrible cries and calls
that the people are calling.
I can hear myself,
mumbling a prayer of hope and light.
I taste my pain as I fearfully open the doors.
I can smell the prejudice in the air
as the wind brisks by me.
I can hear the teens arguing among each other.
I can feel my heart racing a mile a second.
I can feel my fear as I walk down the hallway.
I can taste my sweat as I reach the door
to my classroom.
I can see the teens' eyes look upon me.
I can see my friends from my old school.
I see how upset they are.
I touch my desk and sit in it.
I look and see my teacher through the doors.
I can hear talking to us saying,
"You may not like each other
but you will respect each other."
(Remember the Titans)
I see what the other children feel.
I can remember what my other school was like.
I can hope that this school
is the same as my old school.
Can you see what pain I'm going through?

64

Boy 2:  I can see my mother crying in the crowd.
I can see all my friends' pain,
as we have to share this school with blacks.
I can hear the chants of the crowd
as the school bus gets closer and closer
to the school.
I touch my mom to comfort her
and I tell her everything will be okay.
I can see the African Americans
walking out of the bus.
I can feel their pain.
I can taste my sadness as they walk by me.
I can hear myself, wishing that they
did not have to go through this.
I can taste the crisp air
as the crowd starts growing louder.
I can see the newcomers walking up the stairs
to my school.
I can see a boy look back at the crowd
and mumble something; it seemed like a prayer.
I touch the railing as I go up to my school.
I feel my mom's hand on my shoulder.
I hear her plea for me not to go to school.
I can hear myself telling her everything is okay.
I finally touch the handle to the door.
I can smell the smell of prejudice through the air.
I taste my fear as I walk in mystery
of what is going to happen.
I can see the children arguing.
I wish they would stop.
I can see my friends
as they are talking among each other
and snickering and laughing.

I can see the boy that was praying earlier.
I can see myself walking over to him.
I can hear my friends saying,
"Hey man!  What are you doing?"
I can feel myself trying to understand
what exactly is happening.
I can hear myself say hey to the boy.
I see his body trembling.
I can see his lips move in a prayer.
I can hear myself telling him
that everything is going to be okay
and that I want to be his friend.
I can finally see what pain he is going through.

Lauren McGlory
Age: 13


ANGEL

A ngelic
N ice
G od's creation
E verlasting
L ovely

Quincey Alexander Allen
Age: 12

# CHILDREN OF TODAY

What do you say?
Do you look the other way?
Do you take the time and pray?
I'm talking to you
Children of today
Do you hold your mothers' hands?
Do you ever take a stand?
Do you even have a plan?
Children of today.

Children of today
When you look at the children of yesterday
Do you understand their way?
What they used to say?
What they would play?
Are they now so far away?
Did violence fill their day?

Children of today
Let's find a better way!
To laugh and sing and play
Not violence and dismay
Let's work to bring happier days!
Children of today.

Janay Frances Elinda Duncan

# WISHES

Wishes can be about hate,
Wishes can be about a magic gate.

Wishes are good,
Wishes are great,
Wishes are fun and easy to make.

Wishes are good,
Wishes are bad,
Wishes can even be sad.

Wishes can be about anyone,
or anything.

You can wish to grow up,
You can wish to stay small,
You can even wish to grow tall.

Wishes can be healthy,
Wishes can be wealthy.

Wishes can be about a seed,
Wishes can be about a need.

Wishes can be about toys,
or boys, or even joy.

Wishes can be about vacation,
Wishes can be wished for a nation.

Wishes can be cool,
Wishes can be cruel.

Anthony T. Brown Jr.
Age: 10

## THE PEN

The rope likes to mope,
And the pikes like spikes.
The poor like doors,
But none of them love eating pens
With chocolate icing on top.

Theodore David Baker

## MY GIFT

What can I give him?
Poor as I am.
If I were a shepherd
I'd bring him a lamb.

If I were a wise man
I'd do my part.
Yet what can I do?
I give him my heart.

Keisha Giles
Age: 10


## WE'VE COME TOO FAR TO TURN AROUND

We've come too far to turn around.
We've had our ups and we've had our downs.
We've come too far to turn around,
We had our smiles and we had our frowns.
We've come too far to turn around,
Our life has gained some weights
And lost some pounds.
We've come too far to turn around,
Our life has gone 'round and 'round.
We've come too far to turn around,
What goes up must come down
But, we've come too far to turn around.

D'Angelo Tolver
Age: 11

# THINKING OF YOU

When I open my eyes
to see the sunrise
I think of you.
When I imagine your face
in this wonderful place
I think of you.
When I finally arise
it's no surprise
I think of you.
When I start my day
not far away
I think of you.
When I achieve my goal
I know I'm whole
I think of you.
When I praise your name
I'm not ashamed
I think of you.
When it's time to sleep
it's not really deep
I think of you.
When I say good-bye
please don't cry
because I'll always think of you.

Cortez White
Age: 11

# MOONLIGHT

Look up.
In the sky!
What is it?
It's shining through your window!
You look out your window,
You smile and start to think about
what is happening on the moon!
Are they having a party?
I don't know, you say.
You go to sleep and dream as you usually dream.
You see stars, bright lights, even the Milky Way.
You have landed on the moon.

You think, where am I?

You see unusual creatures dancing.
They are the moonlighters.
Everything is extraordinary.
You have fun with those moonlighters.
The alarm rings.
You wake up.
What a great time you had
On the moon with those moonlighters!

Jodie Sanders
Age: 13

# FRIENDS FOREVER

To laugh with.
To cry with.
To share your deepest frights with.
To help and care about
What ails your aching soul.
To share and dream
What tomorrow may hold.
In rain or shine
Your compassion stays the same.
To walk and talk
And share secret things.
To be with and just knowing
You're always there
Turns the world around.
This dear friend was what you were to me,
So when you went away that day
My world came crashing down.
You were gone
And life wasn't what it used to be
But still I have sweet memories
Of you.
No matter how far away
Whether you go or stay
We will always be
Friends forever.

Dedicated to Ashley D. Sanderson

Joy C. Montgomery
Age: 12

## ROACH, O ROACH

Roach, O Roach,
How can you see
With those big, huge,
Round eyes looking
at me?
O can't you stop
staring
at me?

Daniel Donald Lawson
Age: 12



## AS I STAND

As I stand as a child
soon to be a man.
I glance at the sand
that I walk upon
and think of all the terrible
things that I've done.

As I stand, I should
take things into my own hands
and make them better
and take a chance.
As I stand.

Camaran L. Givens
Age: 12

## THE DAY MY GRANDMA DIED

The day my grandma died
I felt like I was going to cry
I said to myself at night that
she might come back to life. When
I woke up she was not there, I thought
to myself that she does not want to come
back because she is painless where she is and
she had too much pain here because she always
said she wanted new legs, I thought and thought
and finally I knew that she was happy where she
was because she was with her love her husband.

Kristen Evoy
Age: 11


## SAYING GOOD-BYE

A star in the sky
A tear in my eye
When to my best friend I said good-bye
The sights are great
The flowers smell good, but,
I think I should, maybe I might
Put an end to this horrible fight
I said good-bye, I will miss you
But one more question, will you miss me too?

Marissa Caylor
Age: 11

# WE ARE POLLUTERS

We are polluters,
We don't care,
We make messes
Everywhere.
We strip forests
Bare of trees,
We dump garbage
In the seas.
  We are polluters,
  We enjoy,
  Finding beauty
  To destroy,
  We intrude
  Where creatures thrive,
  Soon there's little
  Left alive.
    Underwater,
    Underground,
    Nothing's safe
    When we're
    Around, we
    Spew poisons
    In the air,
    We are polluters
    We don't care.

Miguel Reyes
Age: 10

# I ENJOY...

As you will see
There is no need for TV.
I enjoy biking, basketball, and more.
I like eating pears and apples to the core.
I love reading Roald Dahl.
I like shopping at the mall.
I play I'm in the olden days
Where entertainment's watching plays.
You may say that life hasn't changed
But all our lives are rearranged.
When you have some spare time,
Join me and we'll write a rhyme!

Lucy Wylie - Kellermann
Age: 10

# FLY

Fly,
Fly!
I want to fly in the sky
Where the birds fly
So high, so high
How high can they fly?
Know why?

Frank Daniel Fernandez
Age: 11

77

Pepsi
Tastes wonderful
Good, cool, dark
Ice
Pop

Javier Rivas
Age: 13

## CANDY

Candy is nice and sweet,
  Candy is children's favorite treat.
Candy is good for after a snack,
  I keep a few pieces in my backpack.
Candy is good for after lunch,
  I like to keep a whole bunch.
There are sour Skittles,
  and fruit juice Twizzlers.
There's chocolate candy and fruit flavored too,
  There's even candy that's hard to chew.
Candy is my favorite treat,
  Candy is something people like to eat.

Kenisha Tisdale
Age: 10

# HERE AND THERE

Did you know -- ?
Well why would you care
That I'm over here
And you're over there.

What if we switched
To your point of view?
You will be me
And I will be you.

But I'm still over here
This doesn't seem right
You just watch,
I'll be up all night.

I'll try to figure this out
But it would be grand
If one of us (maybe you)
Could just understand.

And now so you know,
(E'en though you won't care)
I'm still over here
And you're still o'er there.

Johannah Fenton
Age: 13

# THE AGE OF SPRING

Stepping outside into comforting sun,
I discover one world of fantasy.
Far ahead luscious, green meadows run,
And trees are aligned as far as eyes can see.

Newborn fawns try to no avail
Long journeys to the side of anxious mothers,
While countless flowers line forest trails,
Adorning the earth with vibrant colors.

Fresh warm breezes tickle my face
Greeting me from azure skies above.
Soaring through time at its own pace,
Spring arrives and delivers its love.

Amal Killawi
Age: 15


Boy
fine, funny,
playing basketball, going to the mall, teasing
boyfriend/girlfriend
nice, bossy
skating, going to the movies,
talking on the phone
Girl

Veronica Carrion
Age: 14

# ALL THE THINGS I WOULD LOVE TO BE

I would love to be a singer
to share my voice with the world.
I would love to be a racecar driver
to leave the others behind and win.
I would love to be a doctor
and help others when they need it most.
I would love to be a baby-sitter
to care for kids to watch them play and laugh.
And if I could not do that
I would just be out of luck
because I could not share my love with others.

Brittany Alexsandria Lewis
Age: 12


I wish I was a butterfly so I can fly high.
I wish I was a dinosaur so I could roar;
I wish I was a bird but I would not eat worms,
I wish I was a cat
so I won't have to swing a bat,
I wish I was a bluebird
so I could look at bone fishes,
I wish I was a bee
so I would chase down fleas,
I wish I wish to use this rhyme
to go back home until next time.


Jade Jones
Age: 10

# THIS CORRUPT WORLD

We got the President in sin,
Our brother's in the pen,
We got sisters trying to find guys with caddies,
But still can't find their babies' daddies,
We got our mothers cryin',
'Cause their babies' dyin',
Preachers lyin',
Brothers are killin',
Even babies are dealin',
Everybody's just illin',
What's wrong with this
  Corrupt World?

Sabia Duncombe
Age: 15

# CATS ARE

Cats are cute and cuddly,
Except in the muddly.
You wash them
Fluff them
And they are still cute and CUDDLY!

Tiffany Lord
Age: 13

## DRAGONBALL 2

All the Z fighters,
Save the earth
And that is what
The earth is worth.
The forces of evil
Will not prevail,
Because the super-sacen
Are on their tail.
The evil one,
By the name of Cell,
Thinks that he
Will prevail.
Please save the earth!
Please save the earth!
Earth's special forces,
Please save the earth!

Chloé Bohler
Age: 10


## BROTHERS ARE SO ANNOYING!

Brothers, brothers, brothers
SO ANNOYING!
They get what they want,
But I never get
WHAT I WANT!

Amanda E. Saucillo
Age: 10

# VENUS

Every day Venus would play
testing her skills,
going strong, and going on.
Winning titles,
being brave,
being the light shining through the dark cave.
Making a title for women everywhere,
implying we can do it just give us a try,
we can be as good and better than any man.
Courage, determination, and bravery at best
All examples of the characteristics
she possesses.
Just the name itself means something...
something deeper than feelings,
something better than gold,
I think she is rather bold, strong, and smart
and winning Wimbledon was just a start.
There is more in store for this shining star
She is my American Hero, by far.

Dedicated to Wimbledon winner Venus Williams
for her will and determination.

Brittany Williams
Age: 13

# A FAT RAT SAT ON CAT

A cat was being chased by a fat rat.
The cat sat on a trap he set the trap.
The fat rat caught the cat.
The fat rat sat on the cat.
The cat got mad at the fat rat.
The cat ate the fat rat.
Then the cat was a fat cat.

Cody Campbell
Age: 8


# I LIKE WINTER

When the winter comes I like to explore
because there are so many things to do.
I like winter because the air chills my face
as I go sledding down a steep hill.
I like winter because it makes you walk
like the penguins at the South Pole.
I like winter because the snowflakes,
that have no taste, fall on my face.
I like winter because sometimes
there are snow days and I like that very much.
I like winter because when the exploring is over,
it's time for hot cocoa, movies,
and lots of warm covers,
and soon, spring MARCHES IN.

Christopher Boyd
Age: 10

# THE BAT THAT SAT ON THE RAT

A bat sat on a rat.
The rat was angry.
The rat showed his teeth, got all fangy
and scared the bat away.
Then came the cat
who chased
the terrified
rat
all around the room.
The rat got tired
and laid down to rest,
so the cat chewed him up
and said "mmmmm he was the best."
The bat got brave
and floated by the cat.
The cat, who was taking a nap,
woke up
and grabbed the bat out of the air.
The cat was fat and full of food
so he went back to his bed
and
fell
fast asleep.

Gezim Nikaj
Age: 7

## A FRIEND'S DEATH

It broke my
heart to see
you go.  I wish
you could have
stayed another
day.  You couldn't
stay to laugh, to
work, or even to
play.  God called
you to rest
because He knew
best.  In my eyes
you were on earth
a very short while,
but God wanted you
home to finish your
work for Him.  You
were such a good
friend.  Rea, you were
the best of all the rest.
You are in a better place
now.  See you on the other
side.  Good-bye for now.

Jason White
Age: 11

# DEEP BLUE SEA

Any person would fear it,
The sights you'll see in steerage.
Rats, bats, grown men's spats,
They warned, "Go nowhere near it."

But see the great contrast,
'Tween steerage and first class.
The men wear top hats, the women gowns,
Their practiced curtsies quite profound.

But it would come to be,
That they would equal we.
No longer a different class,
Death came with dawn, alas.

There came the big mistake,
The last one they would make.
They tore the bow, lives at stake,
Flooded the cabins and sealed our fate.

The boat came to a halt
'Twas the night watchman's fault.
To sleep he quickly fell,
I tell a horrid tale.

Lifeboats and jackets, none to spare,
Panic-stricken passengers, cold evil glares.
The mountain stood for miles to see,
No land in sight, few able to flee.

Could hear the cries and screams of all,
The splashing of water as they fall.
The frozen water no one tread,
The floating bodies of the dead.

One woman wore a flowing gown,
Was hard to watch that woman drown.
Her family, soon, was taken too
Sinking down into the blue.

Was hard to watch the others die,
And live to see the days go by.
Those who died, went not in vain,
Those that survived recall their pain.

I speak of the Titan of the sea,
Who that night fell upon her knee.
Known as a national tragedy,
When she sank into the deep blue sea.

Erin G. Brantley
Age: 17


## THE MOON

The moon is so bright.
It comes out at night.
It's very far from here.
People think there are aliens on the moon.
But I don't think there are.
I like the moon.

Jeannette Marie Stewart
Age: 7

# I AM

I am a moon
  I brighten darkness
I am love
  because I need it
I am comfort
  on a hard day
I am strength
  because I have it
I am help
  because I give it when it's needed
I am black
I am beautiful
I am intelligent
I am me, myself, and I

Aqweli Parks
Age: 13


# NATURE

Nature is a thing that men cannot bring.
But if they could it wouldn't be called nature.
People don't understand
that nature is not from men
or else it wouldn't be called nature.
As I say again.
Men did not bring nature.

Monet Stokes
Age: 9

# MOMS

Moms are
special in many
ways.
They brighten
up your saddest days.
They make you feel warm
inside.
They cheer
you up when
you start
to cry.
They always
know when you're
feeling sad.
Sometimes
moms make you mad.
Sometimes moms might
call you a little pest.
But you will
always know that
they are the
BEST!!

Aurielle Showalter
Age: 11

My mother made a chocolate cake.
How many eggs did it take?
One, two, three, four, five,
fall in love just like I.
You can't hide from me
and you are going to touch the sky.
One, two, three, four, five.

Rebecca Anderson
Age: 7


## AN ANGEL'S GIFT

An angel left me this feather
and said it was for you.
You must be a special person
if an angel thinks so too.

Amanda Wallace
Age: 12

# SNOW!

Snowflakes are falling,
They are falling everywhere,
It is snowing hard.

Alexander Czarney
Age: 8


# FALL

Fall is when the leaves change colors
like orange, brown, gold and red.

The leaves are so bright and beautiful
if you look at them really close
they look like an orange, a kiwi,
a ring, and a cherry painted on a tree.

Thanksgiving is a part of fall
when you cook a lot for all,
and what a yummy tradition it is.

Fall fall
what a wonderful thing
and after fall
comes winter, and spring.

De Janai Black
Age: 10

## COOKIES

As I walk through my house
it is just me my mom and dad
I have every disability but one
and that is taste
I walk into the kitchen
I can taste my mom's
homemade cookies
well-baked so soft.
So moist but yet so tasty
well-sprinkled with chocolate chips
my warm-hearted mom is a chef
she has awards from end to end
I am forever going to love her
and her cookies until death.

Donavon Turner
Age: 10


## THE WATER

The water is blue.
The water is nice.
The water helps things grow.
The water has dolphins and fish.
Frogs and dogs like the water too.
Water makes trees grow
and the water goes down with the flow.

Travis Daley
Age: 8

G irls
I n the
R oom
L et her
S tay

Thomas Foster
Age: 7

LIFE

Life is not something
you can flow through.
Life is not as easy
as saying I love you too.
Life brings sunny days,
gray days.
Life has its meaning
in its own way.
Life is like a strong blow
of wind.
Life comes again and again.
Life full of tomorrow.
Life is full of goals.
Life as deep as the oceans.
Life always opening and closing.
Life we all have.
Life you receive
and give.

Jessica White
Age: 13

# THE UNFORTUNATE HOMEOWNER

I saw a beautiful shell,
riding on the waves' big swells.
I calmly walked to the sea,
and asked if it could get that shell for me,
the sea laughed many laughs,
and merrily replied that he was very learned,
in the trade of catching shells and rocks,
he signaled for many waves
and they swooped down like hawks,
too late I saw the creature
that lay moaning in the shells,
the waves bashed,
crashed,
and mashed the life out of him,
and in the dim,
moonlight
the waves in their height,
brought the shell to me,
I sadly wept,
over the one who had left,
his abode,
and rode,
the waves to death,
because of me.

Supraja Sharma

# I AM

I am ice-blue
Cool and slick
I am a cheetah
Fast and forever moving

I am Hollywood
Flashy, stunning
I am caviar
Rare and expensive

I am a bonsai tree
A work of art
I am fire
Red-hot

I am a Dodge Viper
Beautiful, powerful
I am an explosion
A loud attraction

I am whatever I say I am,
If I wasn't then why would I say I am?

John Plonka
Age: 13

# THE BOY

The BOY FLIES.    like
A BLUE SHOOTING star
through the BIG BLUE SKY
BoUnCinG and LAUGHING all the while.
GAINING ENERGY from a friendly SMILE.
Suddenly he takes off with a "BANG!!!"
FASTER than a FORD MUSTANG.
SOARING like an EAGLE
above the TALLEST tree.
The boy slows down to feel a GENTLE BREEZE.
He STOPs and FLOATS down.    Like
a HELICOPTER
falling from a GREAT MAPLE TREE.
GRACEFUL in his EVERY MOVE.
That "BOY" is ME.

Paul C. Thomas
Age: 13


For my dad's birthday
We go over to Grandma's
when we go over
we get in our jamas.
Then we have a party
it's really nice.
Sometimes we play with mice
And we have ice cream,
cake and gifts too.

Jermey Parden

## THE THINGS I AM

I am the wisp of the wind,
soothing and calm,
the leaf floating in the air,
light and carefree,
Element of fire prancing high and low,
Tiger of wisdom,
out of seclusion,
a weeping willow
in the breeze,
the maze of confusion,
is my illusion,
I am what I am
as you are you.

Sandy Chu
Age: 13

## THE HOWL

The howl of a lone wolf drifts into the quiet night,
a low mournful cry of despair,
yet a music so simple and beautiful,
it will shatter the icy sky, the crystal stars,
and its ivory target, the moon.
The howl, of a lone wolf.

Lucy S. Gellman

# IDENTITY

Each identity a seashell,
Treasured, unique
Forever changing.
Hidden,
Then suddenly found.
But careful not to break it,
For identities are fragile.

Equal, balanced,
Silent, SWiFT.
Soft, light, and flowing,
Protective, motivational,
Lucky, UNiQUE.

Adventurous, relaxing,
Cool, refreshing,
Elegant.
Soft, yet strong.
Peaceful, yet playful.

Hidden,
Then suddenly found.
But careful not to break it,
For identities are fragile.

Allison Fennell
Age: 13

# THE LOVE I'LL ALWAYS REMEMBER

Sometimes I think about
how you came into my life.

Then when we tried to work things out
but it just didn't go the way we wanted it to go

But knowing when you broke up
I would get over it like I did before,
but I couldn't get over it
the same way I did before
because it hurt me so bad.

Every night I would think about
all the fun things we had done and start to cry.

Then I realized how much you meant to me

Once you found out that you meant much to me
you still didn't care about how I felt
nor did you understand

After all the crying I did.
I understood that you were just another person
in my life and another obstacle to overcome.

LaTerrica Silvers
Age: 14

# KANGAROOS

Kangaroos hop and bop
All the way to the top then drop
They bounce with clowns
They bounce around and around sounds

Mitchel Zaidel
Age: 7

# MY PARENTS

I think I'll keep my parents,
And here are some reasons why.
They help me with my homework,
And make me laugh so hard that I almost die.
They also drive me to school.

They buy me lots of toys,
When I don't make lots of noise.
Then when I ride my bike they make me wear a helmet,
Because they don't want me to get hurt.

They take me to parties,
And make me go to bed so I can get up,
And get to school without getting tardies.
My parents make me happy and that's why,
My parents are good parents.

John Fitzpatrick

# THE SNOW

The snow is falling
Leaves are falling from the trees
Ice is on the ground.

Abbigail Tomasic
Age: 9


# RACING, RACING, RACING

Dirt bike racing
Car racing
Bike, run, swim racing
Four-wheeler, motorcycle, dirty racing
Those are just a few.
Soap box racing
Heavy racing
Good, funny, dirty racing
Bad, stupid, awesome racing
Fun racing, too!
Exciting racing
Fast racing
And don't forget hard racing.
Last of all
Best of all
I like muddy racing.

Rebecca Jones
Age: 9

# THANKSGIVING DINNER

Time for giving thanks
A time for eating turkey
I am so hungry!

Danyele D. Velez
Age: 9

# DOGS, DOGS, DOGS

Furry dogs
Cuddly dogs
Friendly, nice, skinny dogs
Fat, eating, radical dogs
Those are just a few.
Racing dogs
Fast dogs
Slow, small, big dogs
Medium, strange, happy dogs
Sad dogs, too!
Angry dogs
Mean dogs
And don't forget cool dogs.
Last of all
Best of all
I like my dog.

Eric Thompson
Age: 8

# LET IT SNOW

Snow is white and cold
My family went in the snow.
We went back inside.

Tarek Rizk
Age: 9

# MAUREEN

Sparkly pink.
Many UnEVen sides
Moving quickly
Singing brown-eyed girl
Playing it on an oboe
Riding in an adorable blue bug
Sleeping on a fluffy bed overlooking the ocean

I am a graceful birch sapling
Sometimes I breathe fire
I scurry through holes dug by prairie dogs
I have evenness, like the number forty-eight
I am a spicy taco
I lie on a beach for days on end
And never encounter a serial killer.

I am all these things, but alas, only in my dreams.

Maureen G. Kellett

# NIGHT FLIGHTS

Up, around my kite
Wind blows in shadowy heights
My kite will not break.

David Salva
Age: 9

# REVELATION

A next generation springs from our souls
Existing society dictates their roles
As the sun dawns on a New Year
The toasting glasses mask our fear
Revelation comes so near

A dread that our landmarks will disappear
We clamor noisily around to hear
The all faint sounds of little feet
And little faces at the door to greet
Revelation will we meet

Without these munchkins, the house is neat
Though filling the emptiness is quite a feat
In the musty air, listlessness lingers
Walls untouched by chubby fingers
Revelation now malingers

Kathleen Larrabee
Age: 15

# THANKSGIVING FUN

I like Thanksgiving
I can play with my cousins.
We'll play in the snow.

Mark R. Lopez
Age: 8


# THERE'S SOMETHING ABOUT THOSE HOT CHIPS

there's something about those hot chips
is it the flame?
or just the name?
there's something about those hot chips
I'll say it again
I'll say it in vain
I'll do all and all for you
I'll do anything for a box or two
all I want is just one crunch
and maybe a little
munch, munch, munch
all I want is just one bite
oh give me
give me
one more try
if I don't, I won't cry just leave me alone
and let me DIE!!!

Brent McCants
Age: 11

# WINTER IS COMING

The snow is falling.
It is very cold outside.
Trees are blowing hard.

Katie Nicole DiFrancesco
Age: 9

# WHAT IS PLATINUM?

Platinum is the moon, that shines on us.
  Platinum is the star, in the nebula.
Platinum is the prize you have won,
  Platinum reflects the shining sun.
Platinum steals our eyes,
  Platinum never dies.
Platinum, however, is worth more than gold,
  Platinum is wonderful to hold.
Platinum makes diamonds sparkle more,
  Platinum is our choice, the one we adore.
Platinum holds the glitter in place,
  Platinum shows off everything with grace.

John Melonio
Age: 11

## THE FORECAST

Wind wind snowy snow
Tell me what's happening now
Tell me the forecast.

Eric Armbruster
Age: 8

## PUMPKIN PARTY

I got a seed from the store,
but it looked as big as a baby gourd.

I didn't know what kind of seed it was,
so I planted it anyway.
In my backyard.

The next week my mom thought it was a weed.
So she called me out and said
"What is this?"
I said, "It's my seed."

Though I know it looks like a weed,
It grew in a couple months.

One day, I woke up and saw a great orange pumpkin.
That day my family had a great big pumpkin party.

Sara Sanders
Age: 11

# FRIENDS

Friends will be with you right or wrong,
Friends are the ones
That will help you stay strong.
Friends that are faithful, are the best,
Friends are like family,
They will withstand the test.

Friends will come through,
When no one else will,
Friends warm the heart forever still.
So, what can I say,
Friends are like old age wines,
They grow  finer and finer
Through the steps of time.

Steven Shaw

# FROGS

frogs frogs frogs
slimy frogs
cool frogs
bad frogs
what I like
best of all
are
blue frogs

Elizabeth Bandico
Age: 7

# DOGS, DOGS, DOGS

Drinking dogs
Eating dogs
Mean, nice, fat dogs
Inside, outside, ugly dogs
Those are just a few.
Strange dogs
In pain dogs
Sad, happy, cool dogs
Running, walking, jogging dogs
Funny dogs, too!
Skinny dogs
Cuddly dogs
And don't forget exciting dogs.
Last of all
Best of all
I like my dog.

Colin Watson
Age: 9


# WINTER

Snow falls in winter
It might snow on Christmas too
December's the month.

Toni Chavez
Age: 8

# TRULY MYSELF

My Ferrari red
VIBRANT, yet dignified
Three corners of a triangle
Heart
Soul    MIND
All interconnected
I hear the rustling of autumn leaves
As gentle as the sound of a baby's laugh
Seven is my number
Lucky and grateful of it
The peaceful melodies of a violin
play in my head
Being polished and in tune to my inner soul
I am a Ferrari 360 Modena
With a passion for true speed
I AM EARTH
Reliable and always there
To lend a helping hand
You could
Say I am a
R
E
D
wood
NEVER TIMID
And not  h e s i t a n t  to hold my own ground
I am a lighthouse
Beaconing to my followers
To steer clear
Of my rocky shore

There are so many soft, hard, loud,
Peaceful words that can describe me
But don't limit me
To just words...

Robert Cudini
Age: 14

## ISOLATED ROOM

Sometimes I feel like I'm all alone
in an isolated room.
I could be screaming out loud
and no one would even turn a head.
I could be crying
and no one would see the tears I shed.
At times I'm wondering if I belong here.
But it's at those times
that my door to my room opens
and I am welcomed back to the world.
The world that rescues me
from my isolated room.

Amecia Neal
Age: 13

# BEST FRIENDS

Do you know a person
Who's special in a way?
Or do you know a person
Who knows always what to say?

Do you know a person
Who cares of you so much?
Do you know a person
Who your heart they always touch?

Have you ever wondered
Who really, really cares?
And then found a person
Who's always, always there?

Do you stop to think
Who'll be with you to the end?
Well then, stop to call that person
Your very best friend.

Rebecca C. Hodges
Age: 11

# IF I KNEW

If I knew this would be the last time
I'd see you alive,
I'd tell you how much I love you,
And I'd hold that memory close by,

If I knew these would be the last words
You'd hear me speak,
I'd choose them carefully,
And it wouldn't come out weak,

If I knew this would be the last time
I'd ever get to say good-bye,
I'd say it with all my heart,
And hope not to cry,

If I knew this would be the last time
You get to smile and laugh,
I'd take a million pictures,
Just for this memory to last,

And if I knew this would be the last time
I hear you say "I love you,"
I'd hold you close and dear
And I'd say "I love you too"

So make sure to always take the time,
For an extra hug or kiss,
And then you will hold good memories
In your mind.

Jacalyn Metelsky
Age: 13

# BEST FRIENDS

A friend to a preschooler is someone who shares
the blocks with you on your first day.

A friend to a kindergartner is that kid who let you
use their pink crayon to color a picture.

A friend to a first grader is the girl
who walks home with you every day.

A friend to a second grader is the one girl who
sat with you on the bus when no one else would.

A friend to a third grader is the girl
who stuck up for you when you got in trouble.

A friend to a fourth grader is the one who helped
you figure out # 24 on your math homework.

A friend to a fifth grader is the kid
who let you copy their social studies homework
when you forgot to do it.

A friend to a sixth grader
is the girl in your study hall
who tried for weeks to get a detention
so you wouldn't have to go alone.

A friend to a seventh grader is that girl
in science class who walked all the way home
with you when you missed your bus.

A friend to an eight grader is the one person
who always bailed you out when you forgot
to write a report for language arts.

A friend to a ninth grader was the one person
who was willing to listen
to everything you had to say.

A friend to a tenth grader is the person who
always had an answer to all of your problems.

A friend to an eleventh grader is the one person
who convinced you not to drop out
when you thought all was lost.

A friend to a twelfth grader is the girl
who made her senior picture look bad
so yours would look better.

A friend on graduation day is the girl
who stuck by you though thick and thin,
good and bad, and never gave up.
The friend who always listened
and cared about you and what you had to say.

A friend on graduation day is that same person
who shared their blocks with you
on your first day of preschool.

                                    Megan Shoemaker

# THE MEANING OF VETERANS DAY

I thank the veterans of the past,
For I can't remember when
I've thanked them last,
I hope that that I do,
Thank you for the pride and pain
you went through.

It must've been torture,
Sadness by the minute,
To see your house,
Remember the last time,
You stepped foot in it,
Seeing your parents, wife, and child,
Kissing them good-bye
Made your emotions run wild.

Regardless of your feelings,
You had no regrets,
As you prepared for war,
You dripped with sweat,
To yourself you stayed true,
Now is the moment you'll know
What your country means to you.

You fought with pride, and sadness too,
You are struck with pain, a bullet went through,
Your chest is heaving, your breathing slows.
But you're still proud of the path you chose.

Even though your life is through,
We see the flag and think of you,
"Stars and Stripes", we begin to sing,

The red, white, and blue
Will forever reign supreme.

Jessica Siwierka

## THE SNOWFLAKE

The snow is blowing.
A snowflake fell on my nose.
It melted on me.

Nicole Campana
Age: 8

## JEWEL

From spoiled to feeling rotten
My world upside down
Yet, I haven't seemed to have forgotten
The one and only, who's going to be here
Here for me; to help me get out
So many obstacles;
Damien impersonators around

Jewel

Yes, Jewel will make it
All the determination and will power
To grow up, sprout from a seed
To a beautiful flower
I'll show all who failed to believe
I'll never give up faith
You say "Never say Never,"
I say "You don't know me."

One like no other
Nothing like father, so far from mother
I was meant to be..., who?
Somebody,...I know that much.

Jewel

Precious and rare
Fragile yet so strong
This life has proved to be unfair
I am a survivor, will strive to get to the highest
The sky's not my limit; deserving so much more

Impatiently waiting...

Jewel

Yea, that's me
Doing what I do, serving this purpose
For only one
In return: the feeling like I'm on top of the world
Everything happens for a reason
So my life now, could only be building
me stronger

You all will see
Peer pressure doesn't exist
Hard as ice, never able to be brought down
Anything is possible, this is not a myth

Jewel

I better stop writing
For I have a lot to do
To prepare for me,
That everything I've said comes true.

Jewel Romero
Age: 16

# TOYS, TOYS, TOYS

Cool toys
Fun toys
Sweet, funny, exciting toys
Hot, little, gross toys
Those are just a few.
Fat toys
Skinny toys
Nice, swimming, huge toys
Neat, messy, muggy toys
Humongous toys, too!
Small toys
Dirty toys
And don't forget smelly toys.
Last of all
Best of all
I like N'SYNC toys.

Jesseca Horsley
Age: 9


Boy
cool, friendly,
running, laughing, walking,
hanging out together.
Kevin

Kevin Watson
Age: 9

R oses as sweet as me
A wesome
V ery smart
E xciting
N ice

Raven Fairley
Age: 8

## ANIMALS, ANIMALS, ANIMALS

Crazy animals
Bad animals
Rabbit, deer, bear animals
Good, nice, mean animals
Those are just a few.
Snake animals
Little animals
Big, small, fat animals
Skinny, stinky, ugly animals
Cute animals, too!
Tiny animals
Furry animals
And don't forget cow animals.
Last of all
Best of all
I like farm animals.

Angelica M. Quimbaya
Age: 8

# BOYS, BOYS, BOYS

Rotten boys
Spoiled boys
Funny, weird, bald boys
Mean, scared, happy boys
Those are just a few.
Bold boys
Sad boys
Odd, small, big boys
Messy, careless, smelly boys
Mad boys, too!
Baby boys
Funny boys
And don't forget silly boys.
Last of all
Best of all
I like crazy boys.

Faith Gibson
Age: 8

J olly
A wesome
R ich
E xcellent
D aring

Jared Shaw
Age: 8

# DANCING

I dance on wings
Flying, soaring, in the sky,
Right before dancing
I get butterflies,
Golden costumes,
Silver stars,
I start to dance --
Gliding, flying,
Forever and ever,
I dance on wings.

Julie Patricia Novotny
Age: 10

# DECLARATION OF INDEPENDENCE

The Declaration is a symbol of the United States,
It stated our independence which is really great,
July 4, 1776 is when it was passed,
Our thirteen colonies were free at last.

Thomas Jefferson
Was the author of the Declaration,
The result of it was a new nation,
It said that all men were created equal,
The Declaration of Independence
Helped all of the people.

Alyssa Arocho
Age: 13

## THE PROFICIENCY TEST

I studied all year,
and now it's finally here!
It's the first day of the test,
I'll try my best.
The teacher is passing out the book,
I wish I could use the notes I took.
I open the first page,
by the time I'm done I'll be a different age.
I know we studied this,
I think this will be the one I miss.

Eddie M. Carney
Age: 10

## SNOW, SNOW

Snow, snow I love the snow,
Like little people that God has made,
I open my mouth up wide,
And the snow comes in my mouth,
I jump in it,
And get stuck in it,
The snow is even more fun,
Than playing in the sun,
Snow, snow I love the snow.

Ryan Dolan
Age: 10

126

Violence
guns, hitting
shooting, running, hatred
war, killing, harmony, kindness
laughing, playing, jumping
running, free
Peace

Thad McLaughlin

## A DAY WITH GOD

A day when it's bright
I can see God's heavenly light.
I love Him so much,
Sometimes I can feel His lovely touch.
That's a day with God.
I can hear His call,
Without seeing Him at all.
He brings his great presence
With warmness and love,
And with His presence I'm warm and snug.
That's a day with God.
I love God,
Can't you see
A day without God...
Is a day without me!
I know God's a part of me!
This is a day with God!

Christian Schmidt
Age: 10

# PANTHER

You live in a shiny green forest of Africa
Your long and silky tail and fierce, black as night
You look around and feel really small,
looking up at the great blue sky,
smelling around for prey... aha,
you spy a small brown rabbit.
Dashing fast you run after it through bamboo
and tall, tall, trees.  You pounce and miss.
You feel little compared to the trees, and the sky,
but of all animals you are the boss.
King of the forest, you think of yourself.

Amanda Harris
Age: 10

S mart
T errific
E xcellent
P erfect
H elpful
A wesome
N ice
I mportant
E xciting

Stephanie A. Rowen
Age: 8

# DOLPHIN

Dolphin in the deep blue sea,
Swarming in the clear beautiful water.
Being really happy and having lots of fun,
Swimming through the clear, beautiful water,
really fast
Going to the surface, taking a breath,
as free as ever.

Samantha Bennett
Age: 10


## LIFE, LIFE, LIFE

Crazy life
Fun life
Mean, unfair, fair life
Bad, good, dizzy life
Those are just a few.
Blind life
Ocean life
School, nonschool, preschool life
Football, basketball, baseball life
Horrible life, too!
Intelligent life
Happy life
And don't forget exciting life.
But last of all
Best of all
I like ice-cream life.

Joshua Sniezek
Age: 8

# I LOVE SNOW

Snow, snow, I love snow
Everywhere I go
I see it come, I see it go
I love snow.
I love to go ice-skating
or build a snowman too
to hit you with a snowball
is what I like to do
I love snow!

Megan Kiper
Age: 10

# I AM UNIQUE

I am teal, a mix of ENVY and sadness.
I am a sphere, smooth
   and always scanning for edges.
I am a lunge, striking when least expected.
I am a creaking door, ill cared for and loud.
I am a blue whale, large and GRACEFUL.
I am "JETPACK," always ready to go.
I am thirteen, MYSTERIOUS and unlucky.
I am a limo, expensive and good-looking.
I am a beech, always m IxE d up.

Matthew Goodell
Age: 13

130

# RABBIT

A rabbit is a little fluff ball
That hops 'round and 'round,
And nibbles here and there on things,
Even if it's me.

Heather Guenther
Age: 10

# ANGELS, ANGELS, ANGELS

Sweet angels
Nice angels
Good, happy, funny angels
Little, big, cute angels
Those are just a few.
Pretty angels
Sunny angels
Girl, boy, scared angels
Brave, loud, loyal angels
Colorful angels, too!
Night angels
Bright angels
And don't forget smart angels.
Last of all
Best of all
I like fairy angels.

Alexis Segura
Age: 9

# NIGHT FRIGHT

She always had to burn a light
Beside her bed at night.

It gave bad dreams and broken sleep,
But it helped her see the Lord
and her soul to keep.

Good gloom on her was thrown away,
It is on me by night and day.

Who have, as I suppose, ahead
The darkest of it still to dread.

Jessica Mills


# DOLPHINS

She lives in an ocean or even a sea.
She's harmless and pretty as can be.
She swims around as proud as she can in the sea.
There're no sharks in sight,
It's just her and the sea.
She doesn't smell anything, but good.
She sounds cool and soothing.
There are a ton of fish in sight.
She's happier than any other animal around!

Briana Hinz
Age: 10

When I was in eighth grade,
I decided to play football.
I liked playing a lot,
And I was the biggest kid on the team.
I was good.
I played nose guard, middle linebacker
and tailback.
I started every game,
And I would get five or six sacks a game.
Then I got into high school,
And I started there, too.
I had a lot of fun.
I made a lot of friends that year.
At the end of my ninth grade year, I moved.
And then I quit football.
That was the biggest mistake of my life.
And I will regret it for the rest of my life.

Justin T. White


R emember
O nly
S omeone who cares about
E veryone who

H as
A lways
L oved to
L ove

Nicole R. Hall

# PIGS

I like pigs and so do you.
  I like pigs because they're cute.
My parents hate them, I don't know why.
  Leave me alone before I cry.
I want a pig so, so bad.
  SO GIVE ME ONE BEFORE I GET MAD!!!
I drew a picture of a pig.
  She's so funny SHE'S WEARING A WIG.

Faith Chalender
Age: 10


# BUTTERFLY

Butterfly, butterfly
How are you?
Butterfly, butterfly
I'll name you Pooh.
Butterfly, butterfly
I love you!
Butterfly, butterfly
Good-bye too!

Sonya Tilley
Age: 10

## THE STORM'S GIFT

First it sprinkles, then it pours,
Then it will splash outside of your door.
It crashes into the earth,
   as it smashes the ground,
And pounds on the roof,
   what a frightening sound!
It gushes through gutters like blood
   from a deep, painful wound,
But the storm is not over, at least not very soon.
Thunder roars like a vicious, man-eating lion,
And it sounds kind of scary. There's no denyin'.
Shooting down from the sky,
   the bright lightning flashes,
Sometimes burning trees
   and leaving nothing but ashes.
The rain finally slows down,
   and sounds like people mumbling,
And like a giant's hungry stomach,
   the thunder is only rumbling.
The storm moves on to another town,
And eventually everything starts to settle down.
I have made this conclusion: Did you know
The storm is all worth it...
   just to see the rainbow?

Julianne Marie Metzger
Age: 11

# OH NO!

As I awoke,
  In bed I lay.
And I was thinking
  What a beautiful day!

But as I went out,
  Everything was quaint.
The world looked odd.
  I felt as if I would faint.

But I knew
  I had a Father
That would straighten
  Things right out.

So I had no worry,
  Or any reason to pout.

'Cause I knew
  That God would show
What these things
  Were all about.

Evan Harrell

# THE STORM

A black cloud rose at the top at the hill.
Mom was silent and so was Uncle Will.
We heard the noise of the tree next door.
We knew it was coming a storm.
As the wind blew it touched my face.
I knew that it was going to be a chase.
The next thing I heard was Nanny say get down.
It's coming a tornado, it's moving from town.
I ran down the hall with all of my might.
Looks like it's going to be a very long night.
The wind blew the chickens,
the trees and all things on the farm.
The next thing we knew we had lost our barn.
I guess we should be happy we all were okay,
But I'll tell you right now I'll never forget that day.

Amy Lane Stevens
Age: 11


The sun had to shine
So very fine
It had made the sky
Look very lime
I looked in the lake
It seemed very fake
I thought I would fall
And I guess that's all.


Amanda McKeever

# IF THE SUN COULD TALK

If the sun could talk,
Would it talk about the fields of wheat
in Oklahoma, or
Would it talk about the rice paddies
of ancient China, or
Would it tell about the Nazi prison camps, or
Would it tell about the fleeing Hebrew people
from Egypt, or
Would it speak of the places
we could never dream of, or
Would it tell us of the assassinations of J.F.K.,
Martin Luther King, and Ghandi, or
Would it tell us of the ministries of Jesus
and his disciples, or
Would it tell of the Son of God
being crucified on the cross, or
Would it tell of all the strife and despair
in Serengeti, or
Would it cry about the nuclear bomb
on Japan, or
Would it tell us about ancient times
and how the Egyptians built the pyramids, or
Would it help us understand the mysteries
and vastness of space, or
Would it tell us of the depths of the ocean,
where we have never been, or
Would it tell us of our own existence
and how God made the world, or
Would it tell us how to be at peace
with our fellowman, or
Would it teach us to know and respect
the earth and nature, or

138

Would it remind us of our miseries
through the years, or
Would it praise us
for our mighty triumphs of time, or
Would it be silent as if it couldn't talk.

Benjamin Cory Duncan
Age: 12

## THE GREAT SNAKE

Hi. I am a snake.
I really like to eat mice.
They are so tasty.

Jacob Pleban
Age: 8

# HOW I LOVE THAT WINTER DAY

Winter day, winter day.
How I love that winter day.
How I love that pretty white snow.
How I love it nipping at my toes.
How I love to drink hot cocoa.
How I love to pretend in the snow.
How I love to make snow angels.
How I love to go ice-skating.
How I love that sweet winter day.
How I wish it would never go away.
Now I have to wait for another sweet winter day.

Shakelia Miller
Age: 11


I feel a chill in the cold night air.
It feels as if I am bare.
What is it that I seek,
Away in the depths of my sleep?
Do I seek wisdom, seek faith?
What do I yearn to find in the human race?
But alas!  This is all my weary dream
And no one will hear me when I scream
But what is it I'm screaming for?
Is it the raven?
Quoted no more?

Shannon Finn
Age: 12

# THE JUNGLE

The jungle
a beautiful place
home of the hidden
home of the predators
when night comes
the hidden awaken
they come out
and the predators
pounce
finish their prey
as the sun beats down the night
the surviving of the hidden
go back to their spots
then night awakens again
the hidden come out
and start the circle of life
all over again

Phillip Lee Fugate
Age: 12


# BEAUTIFUL

Your love is like a lily
that blossoms in the spring,
and your voice is like bells
ringing "you and me."

Bret McIntosh
Age: 10

# KITTY

My kitty's name is Baby
she's cute and sweet and lazy
but when I get home
and talk on the phone
she really can drive you crazy
she's mean and cuddly
and more than a little fuzzy
when she lays down
she curls all around
and sleeps with my buddy

Marty Patrick
Age: 12

# THE CAT SAW A RAT

A cat saw a rat
and the cat
was very hungry
so he gobbled the rat
a dog that had a rumbly tummy
saw the fat cat
so he munched him right up.

Michael Ballard
Age: 8

# KEITH ALAN

My cousin Keith Alan
he's one of a kind.
All he does is ride, ride, ride
on a four-wheeler
We did everything together.
He was
My favorite cousin
My four-wheeler buddy
My friend.
When he died it felt like
the world
stopped spinning.
The flowers stopped blooming.
The wind
stopped blowing.
We were are close as clouds
and the sky and
He will always be in my heart
forever.

Vanessa Renee Slone
Age: 11

# MY IMAGINARY PLACE

No one has ever seen my
Imaginary place
   That's because,
It's in my imagination
There're yellow daisies all around me
dancing in the wind
   that comfort me
The sunshine shines down on my face
like an angel opening its wings to
take me to Heaven.
   The grass grasps me and holds
me tight
     and it takes away all my bad
thoughts.
  I like this place because,
   I can sit and be calm,
let my thoughts and dreams fly with
the wind.
  This place is always inside of my mind
   when I'm
     mad
      or
    sad
   I can always count on
this place to comfort me

Elise Collins
Age: 11

# AUTUMN LEAVES

Autumn leaves, as pretty as a rainbow,
But in hues as deep as the setting sun.
Lovely, glowing leaves, welcome!
Your stay will be short,
But you give my world a colorful look!

Elizabeth Schick
Age: 8


# SNOW

Snow, snow is everywhere
over here and under there.
Snow is white and fluffy too,
and sometimes snow is thrown at you.
Snow is cold and really wet
and will always be like that I bet.
Snow is fun when you play,
but it's not fun at the end of the day.
Snow turns to ice when the day is done,
and that's when the snow is no longer fun.
Snow only comes once a year,
and that's when all our parents fear.
Snow makes it harder to drive
to get to where they want to arrive.
I like the winter, it's my favorite season
and I can give you one good reason...
SNOW!!

Richard Clark
Age: 10

# THINKING SPOT

I have a thinking spot that hugs me
like a giant monster.
It is my sunshine on my down days.
This very place is where I can run to,
it is like my best friend.  It is my best friend.
I can talk to it and it talks back,
but not in words, in emotions.

I often lie back in the old computer chair,
staring at the computer screen.
While wild visions of my imagination
fly through my mind.

I will stare down at the old dirt crackled carpet,
looking at all of the surroundings,
surroundings that are special to me,
surroundings like paper,
speed drills, posters, crumbled paper.

Sometimes I close my eyes
and I can feel the scent of rotten candy,
surrounding me like a prison.

But sometimes I don't smell, look or anything,
I only think.
I close my eyes and try to make out
all the blurred visions,
blurred visions of the classroom.

The happy times of the classroom,
times like me flipping over in my chair.
Times when all the children were smiling,
and you could see the happiness
and joy in their eyes.

Finally I make out all the blurred visions
and a tear of joy streams down my face,
and finally I figure out why God led me
to that old room in the first place,
He just wanted me to be happy,
and He wanted me to be thankful
for all the good times that I did have in that room.

Megan Mosley
Age: 10

## HAPPINESS

Happiness is the color of blue skies
It sounds like your favorite jazz song
It tastes like pizza
And smells like blossoms in the early morning
Happiness looks like a daisy in the afternoon
When you touch it,
You feel like you're in Heaven.

Fayez Khalil

147

The feel of my hand in my glove
This is the feeling that I love
I can always hear the crack of the bat
It doesn't matter where I am at
I take in everything that is around me
Once you've seen it you know you've found me
The smell can take my breath away
I am there almost every day
So when I chew my gum, the gum I wield
I know I am at the baseball field

Brian Sizemore


## MEMORIES OF THE OCEAN

This summer I went to the ocean.
I remember while lying
on Mother Nature's hot sunny beach,
I heard the master calling my name,
Nikki, Nikki, Nikki
to come and rejoin all of the other kids!
So I obeyed the huge body of land mass,
and went to join the rest of the kids.
When I had gotten in I recall that the master
felt like my father's arms wrapping around me
at my birthday.
That is my memories of the ocean.

Nikki Lynn Ritchie
Age: 12

# TAKE A STAND FOR A DRUG FREE LAND

Why do people do drugs?
I don't understand,
They blacken your lungs
And kill you man!

Smoking, drinking and drugs
Are the worst things you can do!
For yourself
And other people too.

Just say no!
I dare you to be drug free.
It's best for health,
Can't you all just see!

I'm telling you now,
You must take a stand!
We need to make this country
A drug free land!

Mark Schadler
Age: 11

# DREAMS

Are your dreams hallow?
Open to fly free like a sparrow

Golden hills and silver streams
Carousels are in your dreams

Are your dreams hallow?
Open to fly free like a sparrow

Meeting people from the past
Wishing that one kiss will last

Are your dreams hallow?
Open to fly free like a sparrow

Facing your fears beyond its height
Hearing one last shrill of fright

Now are your dreams still hallow?
Open to fly free like a sparrow

Now your dreams are at a temptation
Finally able to rely on sensation

Walata L. Cobbs
Age: 13

# WINTER RAIN

When you walk in winter rain,
Do you ever think of winter pain,
When the rain is really cold,
Do you think of frostbites,
You can't wait to do April kites!!

So go home to your little sisters,
And ask them if they could play the game
Called Fisher's,
Then wash up for bed,
And have nice warm dreams,
And have nice dreams,
About the color of Christmas greens.

Taylore Che

There once was a big hairy dog
and he lived in a big hollow log
He looked for a friend
He found the end
And there was a big hairy frog!

Brittany Renee Crowder
Age: 9

# FALL

Leaves of purple, red and yellow
Gathered from the trees by a fellow,
Jumped in by children like me and you
Then swept away by the wind so new.

The wind is growing
The leaves are blowing,
It sounds as if it could be snowing
But it is only the wind bellowing.

Flowers are dying
The wind is crying,
Winter is coming
The flowers are crumbling.

Kateri Sparough
Age: 12

# FISH

She swims
She eats
She plays
She jumps
She dies.

Kelly Cooper
Age: 9

## WINTER THOUGHTS

I look out my window and what do I see?
A soft world of snow that's smiling at me!
It's white and it covers the earth no mistake,
And I think to myself,
"This I won't have to rake!"

I see the snowmen built by kids down the street,
And their hands, I do think must be red as a beet!
The nice wet galoshes will thaw in the hall,
And I think, "This will all be over in fall."

I make myself pots of tea, oh so warm,
And say to myself, "I will come to no harm."
My fireplace crackles, so warm and so red,
And reminds me
That maybe not all things are dead.

Alexandra E. Ogden
Age: 13

## SUMMER SHINE

The flaming sun, so harsh on the waves.
The water pounding in a furious rage.
The boiling sand, swept through the air.
The wind whistling through the ocean so fair.

The glistening light of the summer's array.
The feeling I have on a glorious day.
The sea gulls soar heavenly
Through the crisp sky blue.
I feel in the air, the fresh morning dew.

The palm trees sway, as they long to have life.
Its leaves pierce the air,
Like a just sharpened knife.
This is the image you see, when summer's begun.
The three months awaiting you
Are filled with fun!!

Emma Rose
Age: 11

## HALLOWEEN

Orange, brown, yellow, red
Autumn is getting near.
All the trees start to shed
Halloween is here.

Jack-o'-lanterns flicker
Kids go trick-or-treat.
KitKats, Twix, and Snickers
They're all fun to eat.

At the abandoned shack
Enter if you dare.
Monsters will attack
So you better be aware.

Jason Pittinger
Age: 14

# FALL

During fall it gets colder,
The life around gets so much bolder,
And as this happens the colors turn,
They look as though they are going to burn.

The children can't wait to go trick-or-treating,
To get the candy they are seeking,
They dress up and get candy from hosts,
The scary costumes are goblins and ghosts.

People's houses they decorate,
For Halloween, we can hardly wait
With spider webs and spiders crawling,
Afterwards it can be quite boring.

Julie Rose
Age: 13

# SPRING

Why is it every spring
the birds begin to sing?
Why is it every spring
a bird is on a wing?

Why is it every spring
it looks like it will snow?
Why is it every spring
the wind will always blow?

Why in spring
do I think I can fly
that if I will reach up
I'll touch the sky?

Why in spring
do I think night and day?
I should spread my wings
and fly away.

Marsalis W. Burgin
Age: 13

## SUMMER STARS

Shining glittering,
Stars sparkle softly in the
Summer's midnight sky.

Ashley Haring


## THE SUMMER DAY WE MET

The summer heat made me feel sticky,
The stickiness made me feel icky.
The overwhelming summer heat,
I'm telling you, was not too sweet.

In the swimming hole I like to swim,
I like to swim there with my friend, Jim.
That summer made me feel too hot,
But I'm telling you, the pool was not.

The summer sun was very hot,
It was hotter than a boiling pot.
It was so hot it made me sweat,
And that describes the day we met.

Ashley Laura Riesenberg
Age: 12

## THE BLUE JAYS

The blue jays are out,
They are chirping so loudly,
The sound fills my ears.

Miles Foisy

## KIDS' DAY

I wish there was a day called Kids' Day,
and if there was such a day
there would be no school so the kids could play.
Although the teachers are sad,
The kids can have fun.
The young kids could say,
Daddy let's go play with my favorite ball today.
While the older kids would say,
what a boring day today.
All the adults would say,
I wish the kids were in school today.
That's why I wish
there was a day called Kids' Day,
because the fathers and mothers have a day.

Megan Tolliver

# CHEROKEE

In the deep, dark forests,
Of the Eastern Woodlands
Lived a tribe of Indians,
Called the Cherokee.

As the sun rose above,
and the animals began to stir,
So did the Cherokee Indians.

They farmed the land,
In which they lived,
For the soil was rich and had much water.
They hunted and fished and gathered food.
And they loved the land as much as their lives.

At powwows, they celebrated their god,
"The Great Spirit"
Who blessed them with food, shelter, and health.
Much like our God or Jesus today.

When the pale-faced men
Crept out of their ships to steal the land
from the Cherokee.
All they wanted was peace,
But soon the Cherokee went to war
to claim the land was theirs.
But the Cherokee lost the wars
for they had bows and arrows
and the white men had many more soldiers
and powerful guns.

They cut down the forests
that rightfully belonged to the Cherokee
for their pastures and homes.
They polluted the rivers and air.
They didn't care what they did to the land
where the Cherokee had lived,
As long as they had their way.
And many white men that I know,
are still the same way today.

LeeAnna Jade Stewart


## KITTENS

Some are gray,
Some are white,
Some are black;
Black as night,
Some are spotted
others not,
Some are skinny,
Some are fat,
Some are friendly,
others not one bit,
But most of them
just lie around
sleeping,
I don't know why
They call them cats,
But that's a good question
To ask the vet.

Krystin Carlson

# ONE LAST WONDER

Daylight puddles on the brink of the horizon,
All stills as the world waits...
For one last wonder before darkness befalls them
And God pulls out His pallet
And prepares to paint.

Angels spread a canvas of perfect sky,
God dips His paintbrush into reddish hues;
Splashes of gold and ripples of purple
Against a background of pastel blue.

In tranquil repose the world gazes --
The hubbub quieted, the action slowed.
Through every soul a rush of amazement
As the western sky before them glows.

Then God pulls a blanket of nightfall o'er them --
Tucking the world down to rest
And all sleep soundly in knowing, tomorrow,
They shall witness God's last wonder again.

Heather Nicole Salyers
Age: 15

# THANKSGIVING

I sit and gaze upon,
the passionate orange of the pumpkin pie,
the scrumptious brown of the turkey,
the golden corn,
the delicious, mouth-watering, fresh green beans.
Sweet potatoes to die for,
mashed potatoes gently glazed in butter.
It's nearly perfect.
I just can't wait.

Brittany Dudley
Age: 10

# FLOWERS

Rows of tiny plants
Blossoming in the garden
Hoping for some life.

Genna Muriello

'Twas the night before Christmas
And all dressed in black
Was a really mean burglar
With a big black sack.
Christmas came the night after that.
He wore a really old hat that looked just like a cat.
He picked the lock of a very large house
Just then out ran a mouse.
He made a really weird sound
And he started to look around.
Out ran the owners of this very large house
And just then he felt like he was in a blouse.
He thought for a second
Then tried to explain that he was only lost
But they weren't buying
And just realized that soon he might be dying.
He tripped over his shoes
(In a basketball game
That would get a lot of boos).
Just then he saw the mouse that ran out the door
It bit him on the nose and started to pose.
He ran away and started to scream
Then he woke up it was only a dream.
He went and gave money to all.
Then went back to his house
And started to scrawl.
From there on in he vowed never to steal again.
Now he lives admired by all
In his nice little house
With his small pet mouse.
So if you ever pass his home in London, England
You will know he's there
Because he will be telling his stories to all.

Derrick Carper

Eyes are a window to someone's heart
The place where pain and tears start
The place where life may seem to end
The place where life begins again

Eyes are a window to the soul
The place where enchanted dreams are sold
The place that brings inspiration in
The place where love comes from within

Eyes tell the truth
They cannot lie
They always have spare tears to cry
They know there's always something
That's gone wrong
They teach you how to move along

Eyes are a window to someone's heart
Maybe one day you'll look in my eyes

Talia Markley Amatulli




Beautiful ocean
Wonderful, beauteous, waves
Marvelous ocean

Anjana Kumar
Age: 9

## SEASONS

The snow falls slowly down
Until it hits the ground.
Then the wind begins to blow
And the snow gets flown around.

At the haunted house
Enter if you dare.
When you get in there
You'll find a scary mouse.

I run through the leaves
I jump into the mound.
The leaves fly up
And are blown all around.

Evan A. Sexton
Age: 14


W olf
O utside in the dark
L ooking for people to play with
F or a good time.

Cheri Lewis
Age: 9

Spring
A time to hear the little birds sing
Thank heavens that it's finally spring.
Life is showing everywhere
From a budding tulip to a newborn hare.

Summer
I think of the pool
Where we splash and play,
A place to keep cool
On a hot summer day.

Winter
As I go outside
I hear the wind blowing;
I look to the sky
And see the heavens snowing.

Michael Vollman
Age: 13


I saw a rabbit
The rabbit was playing ball
I was quite amazed.

Lucas Kenbeek
Age: 8

# A PANDA

A panda lives in a beautiful rain forest,
Covered with greens,
Flowers and trees,
A panda, black and white,
Not too white, maybe even gray,
Its eyes filled with fear,
It thinks poachers are near,
And coming for him.
And stops along on all fours,
Climbing trees,
Trying to escape the approaching danger,
Through bushes and flowers,
Not noticing anything else,
Its mind stuck on going forward,
Escaping,
Going as fast as he can,
Still filled with fear,
He walks along.

Marissa VonGunten
Age: 11


D eer
E at lots of carrots
E scape from hunters
R un away

Sara Marie Hanley

# MY FAVORITE PLACE TO VISIT

My favorite place to visit,
I go there all the time.
I can go there all the time,
Because my favorite place to visit,
Is in my mind.

In my mind, I can go there any time.
For a short time or even a long time.
But mostly I go there in my spare time.

My mind is my favorite place to visit.
Because only I can decide what will happen.
And only I can make it happen.

In my mind, there is no color, no size or shape.
And there is definitely no hate.
For to visit my mind, I will never hesitate.

My favorite place to visit,
I go there all the time.
I can go there all the time,
because my favorite place to visit,
Is in my mind.

Angela Clark
Age: 11

# WIND

The wind blows
gently through my hair.
A slight breeze cools me off.
O, for without it life would
be so boring.
Thank you wind.
Please come back tomorrow and the next day
and forever and ever again.

Matthew Tyler Wells

There once was a lake
Which was formed by a quake
That was caused by three frogs
Who sat on some logs
They had a lot of fun
While playing in the sun
They hopped on a tree
And paid the squirrel a fee
Then they came and played with me.

Nicholas Andre Youngstrom
Age: 10

## MOMS

Moms are as beautiful as crystals
They are as sharp as bristles.
Their eyes are as bright as stars,
Their cheeks, as red as Mars,
Their hair smells as good as flowers,
Moms, well, they have the power.

Cassandra Gosche
Age: 10


## WHITE TIGER

In the jungle that runs free,
White tigers as beautiful as can be.
Their blue eyes shimmer in the sky
when the sun is up day and night,
when they're looking for food and prey,
They swiftly and quietly get them that day.

Virginia Schaeffer

## SOUNDS

Birds chirping in the trees.
Kids playing in the leaves.
Trees swaying in the breeze.
Cars speeding with ease.
The flag flying in the wind.
Planes that soar again and again.
These are the sounds I love to hear.

Matt Redford
Age: 12

## CHRISTMAS

I love Christmas.
Christmas rules, I think.
That's only my opinion.
Oh, Christmas is fun.
Oh, yeah snowy old
Christmas is fun.

Kendra Dawn Elliott
Age: 10